SECRETS OF A MASTER CHEF

Basic Rules & Shortcuts

To
Charlie
Le grand chef au T.V.
Bon Appetit
François

SECRETS OF A MASTER CHEF

Basic Rules & Shortcuts

by
Master Chef
François Sigrist

Averette Publications, Inc.
Austin, Texas Las Vegas, Nevada
http://www.treasurebook.com

Published in the United States of America
by Averette Publications, Inc.

http://www.treaurebook.com

ISBN 0-9660340-3-1

Special Sales Director
Averette Publications, Inc.
P. O. Box 685069
Austin, Texas 78768

Printed in the United States of America

Special Thanks To:
r.davis design - Cover Design
D. Mitchell - Text Design
C. Allison - Copy Editing

First Edition

GLORIOUS FOOD

Food is the single most important ingredient in our lives. Not only does our survival depend on our physical consumption of food, but our obsession is also evident in the amount of time we spend thinking about it, talking about it, planning for it, and consuming it.

Food is our joy and our sorrow. It satisfies our hunger and is a part of all our special events — a wedding perhaps, or a birthday party, an anniversary, a funeral, a cookout with friends, a family reunion, a gathering to watch a sports event on TV, or a romantic picnic. We include food when we are trying to impress someone, to get a promotion, a raise, a lucrative contract, to get an important client or keep one. We use it to lure a date, to create an intimate moment, and even to compliment a voluptuous occasion in our lives. We use it to combat loneliness, sadness, and boredom. We eat out of hunger, lust, taste, and relish. We don't need an excuse. We are consumed by it — where to eat, when to eat, and with whom we are going eat when we finally choose a place. Whether we eat at home or at a restaurant, we still have to decide what to eat. Finally with the food in front of us we grab our knife, fork, spoon or any appropriate device, and we stuff our faces while worrying about eating too much, our calorie intake, or who is going to pay the bill.

Then we have more decisions about when to stop. "Dessert anyone?" "How about coffee?" "Have a cookie. They just came out of the oven." Next, we are wondering why we ate so much, while massaging our stomachs, regretting the intake under heavy breathing.

Don't despair. Mother Nature will help out. In less than six hours you will be back with your head in the fridge, wondering what is there to eat since your stomach has been nagging you for the last couple of hours.

Oh, glorious food, I dedicate this book to you.

INTRODUCTION

For many years my friends, family, and peers have asked me to write a cookbook. I have resisted for the simple reason that there were already too many books out there on the subject. But they continued to hound me saying, "You have cooked for royalty, dignitaries, movie stars, sports celebrities, and even fellow chefs have called you for advice on blending flavors." So I gave in, sat down, and started writing in longhand.

Cooking is mainly an affair of the heart. I have included stories from my past which I hope will entertain you and inspire you to just get in the kitchen and do the best you can. Let your heart and imagination take over. Do not think of my book as a recipe book, but simply as a tool to spark your imagination and build your self-confidence. Have a sip of coffee between chopping and stirring. Listen to music while you are creating. The more relaxed you are, the better the food will taste. Have your loved ones participate letting them taste the food, set the table, or just keep you company.

You will see that there is leeway to exercise your own personal taste in most of the measurements given in the recipes that I have included. Think of yourself as a "Merlin In The Kitchen" with the freedom to add more of your favorite spice or less of something that disagrees with your stomach. Baking requires a strict adherence to amounts listed since the chemical interaction of the ingredients is critical. Have you ever had a cake fail to rise? The reason that most chefs do not like to bake is exactly what I have described — they want or actually demand the freedom to create! I extend that opportunity to you, and I hope that my book will be of help as a general guideline.

I guess I have cooked for someone every day of my adult life as if it was a special occasion. I have put the same effort into my creations whether they were for the Queen of England and Ronald Reagan or for my local plumber (actually he's more important since I value his skills and see him more often) and *pour moi* (myself). So keep in mind how important the people are who will eat your creations beginning with yourself and your family, and you will never go wrong.

Have fun! I will be right there looking over your shoulder giving you advice throughout your affair. *Bon Appetit!*

Your personal chef,

François

MENU

Basic Facts, Techniques, And Tips

BASIC EQUIPMENT FOR YOUR KITCHEN

When I had my catering company I was amazed at how poorly many of the private kitchens were equipped. Of course I carried my own pots and pans, utensils, and equipment, but occasionally I would need an extra towel or spoon and was unable to locate an appropriate substitute. Even experienced cooks told me, "I did have a whisk, but my daughter loved to play with it when she was small. I guess I threw it away when it got bent." So I have created a list of items that will make cooking faster and easier.

- ☑ Different size wooden spatulas and spoons, at least 6 or 8
- ☑ 2 rubber spatulas, one small and one large
- ☑ 2 ladles, one for gravy and one for soup
- ☑ Skimmer or slotted spoon to remove vegetables from liquid
- ☑ Colander
- ☑ 2 strainers, one small and one large
- ☑ 2 whisks, one small and one large
- ☑ Measuring cup
- ☑ Mixing bowls, 3 to 4 different sizes (stainless steel is best for mixing and glass for storage)
- ☑ Clean towels, at least 6 to 8
- ☑ Pot holders
- ☑ Can opener
- ☑ A set of knives, at least 4: a paring knife, a 10-inch chef's knife, a general-purpose knife, and a serrated knife
- ☑ A peeler
- ☑ Pepper mill for fresh ground pepper
- ☑ Scissors to be used in the kitchen only
- ☑ A meat fork
- ☑ Tongs
- ☑ A hand mixer
- ☑ Pots and pans (You can never have too many but

start out with at least 3 sizes of covered pots and a covered skillet)

- ☑ Glass casserole dish with lid
- ☑ Set of air-tight containers for refrigerator
- ☑ Grater

FOR BAKING

- ☑ 2 baking brushes so that you can always have one clean and dry
- ☑ A scale to weigh your ingredients
- ☑ Flour sifter
- ☑ Rolling pin
- ☑ Cookie sheet
- ☑ 2 round or square cake pans
- ☑ Rectangular baking sheet

None of these items are vital, but the right tool sure does save time and energy.

Allspice: (also called Jamaica pepper) Used in the preparation of homemade sausage, pickles, fish, relishes, and desserts. I don't like it, so use it at your own risk.

Anise: Not of great use in your kitchen. It is used mainly in the liqueur and bakery industries, and you may find it listed in a cookie or candy recipe.

Basil: This herb goes well in meat dishes or salad dressings.

Bay Leaves: Use these in your meat stews, lamb dishes, soups, and tomato dishes. Remove and dispose of bay leaves before serving.

Burnet: Use to season soups, sauces, vegetables, and fish dishes. It tastes a little like cucumbers.

Caper: One of my favorite condiments. It has distinct taste and goes well in tartar sauce, meat balls, and over fish.

> For best results add the capers in sauce, salad, or as a garnish to the finished product.
> DO NOT COOK!

Cayenne Pepper: Good as an all-around lifter for spicy dishes, but don't put too much. It is always easier to add more than put too much and be sorry.

Chervil: Soups and salads are two of the dishes that benefit from this glorious herb.

Chives: Great in soups, salads, fish dishes, cream cheese, omelettes, and for decoration.

Cinnamon: A must for all kitchens. Good in compotes, hot beverages, preserves, fruits, cookies, pastries, bread pudding, etc.

Coriander: You might use the seeds in pickles and the ground in cakes, pastries, and gingerbread.

Cloves, whole: For pickles, marinades, game.

Cloves, ground: In cakes, pastries, cookies, hot punches, bread.

Curry: If used sparingly curry to me is one of the finest spices in life. Use it in sauces for chicken, fish, lamb, and many vegetable dishes.

Dill: Really adds to sauces for fish.

> For best results do not cook fresh herbs. Add to sauce at the last minute and stir.

Garlic: No introduction or explanation is necessary. It will simply make your food sing. I love it in soups, sauces, vegetables, and meats, and it can even lower your cholesterol I'm told. I just adore the flavor.

> Garlic should be cooked at a lower heat than onions, celery, mushrooms, etc. Therefore, add the garlic after the onions, etc. are adequately cooked. It will get bitter if overcooked.

Ginger: Perfect in many of your Chinese dishes and also for soups in cold weather.

Horseradish: Fresh horseradish is good on fish and prime rib. It is available dried or in jars.

Marjoram: Try it in potato soup, meat dumplings, herb

sauces. Store in sealed container.

Mint: Fresh or dried, it is good in beverages, on lamb, and as a decoration for many desserts (fresh leaves only). Mint is also found in sauces and even ice cream.

Nutmeg: You've probably tasted it in eggnog, pudding, custard, and other desserts. But it is also excellent in mashed potatoes, Brussels sprouts, mushroom, and spinach dishes.

Onions: No kitchen should be without onions. (Dried should be used only in dire emergencies in my opinion.) To be on the safe side just buy them every time you go to the grocery.

Oregano: A must in Italian cooking–sauces, salads, pizza, and pastas. Also found in Greek and Mexican dishes.

Paprika: A wide array of uses in food from enhancing the taste to decoration. Use on potatoes, fish, egg dishes, meat stews, goulash, salads, and soups.

Pepper: Black raw pepper is used to flavor many foods. Most vegetables should be peppered after they are cooked. White pepper is the same taste as black. Most chefs prefer the white since it does not show in *Bechamel*, *Alfredo*, and other light dishes.

Rosemary: Absolute dynamite on pork, lamb, poultry, and in soups.

Sage: Primarily used in poultry stuffing.

Tarragon: Personally I think of it as a little taste of heaven in my kitchen. Put in sauces for chicken or fish and soups.

Thyme: If you don't have it in your kitchen, you are losing major points in the flavor game. Get the rubbed leaves only.

(The ground has no place in my kitchen.) Use it in soups, sautéed mushrooms, sauces, quiches, shepherd's pie, meat sauce, steak, kidney pie, chicken, etc. In Provencal and Italian cooking the dishes are too numerous to list. I would go so far as to say, "With no thyme in your kitchen, there is no joy in your food."

Vanilla: A necessity for baking.

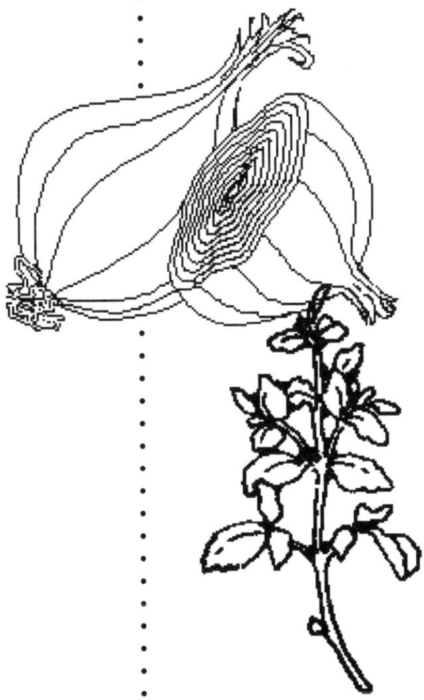

- ☑ Keep a fire extinguisher in the kitchen, but away from the stove area.
- ☑ Keep the hood over the range clean from accumulated grease.
- ☑ Open and ventilate gas ovens for a few minutes before lighting them up.
- ☑ Use only dry, clean hot pads when taking things out of the oven or off the surface burners.
- ☑ Stir with a long-handled spoon. Remove it from the pan when not in use.
- ☑ Stand back when opening pressure cookers. Follow manufacturer's instructions.
- ☑ Lift the lid on the side of the pan directly opposite of you to let the steam escape.
- ☑ Keep the handle of pans away from the source of heat.
- ☑ Move slowly with full containers to avoid splashing.
- ☑ Warn your family and guests when china is hot.
- ☑ Do not overfill pans with liquid; even simmering tomato sauce has a tendency to splash.
- ☑ Do not drip water over hot pans.
- ☑ Strike matches away from you.
- ☑ Keep a supply of salt to stop oven fires. Sprinkling it on grease will soak up the excess.
- ☑ Keep small pets out of the kitchen. It is easy to trip over them, especially when you are moving large objects and cannot see them.
- ☑ Small children should be in appropriate furniture at a safe distance from the heat-producing appliances. Even the outside of the door to the oven can burn a small hand.

KNIFE SAFETY AND CUT PREVENTION

- ☑ Straight knives are primarily used for chopping.
- ☑ Serrated knives are more useful for the novice cook. They stay sharp much longer.
- ☑ Always keep your knives sharp. If they are dull, you are more likely to lose patience. You press harder and bang — the knife goes flying through the cabbage and nips your finger. A sharp knife is a better bet.
- ☑ Never leave a knife in the sink.
- ☑ Never leave a knife in children's reach.
- ☑ Never leave a knife on the counter. If you cover it up with a lid or towel, it is an unpleasant surprise when you grab the towel, encountering the blade.
- ☑ Store knives in the proper place in a knife block or knife drawer.
- ☑ Never use a knife to open lids, caps, cans, or other things.
- ☑ Use the proper tool.
- ☑ Hold knives by the handle.
- ☑ Cut away from your body, and use a cutting board. If the cutting board is slippery, put a flat, moist towel underneath for a better grip.
- ☑ Pay attention to the job when cutting. Do not get distracted.
- ☑ Chips of glass or china should be disposed of properly. Do not just put them in a trash can. First put them in a box or container since plastic bags can tear and cans could be turned over.
- ☑ Drain water from the sink before removing broken china or glass. Water distorts distance.

CONFIDENCE-BUILDING TIPS FROM THE CHEF

1. Never make excuses for the taste of food. As a chef I have heard too many times, "It does not taste the same as the last time," or "It tasted better when Grandma made it." Stop right there.

   How can your guests, family, or friends compare it to the last time or to your grandma's cooking? Besides, the prepared food companies don't ever ask how you like it. They condition you before you even try it that it is the best you have ever had. It is not opinion that matters, but convincing you that it is good and you will love it. Put the food on the table and say, "Man, it tastes great. I just tried it in the kitchen." Chances are, they are going to salivate well before they can dig their silverware into it.

2. Never apologize. What for? Like the others, you have been working all day. They should be happy there is food on the table. Some key phrases I find soothing are: "You know where the fridge is if you don't like it." or "Why don't you cook?" or "You don't have to stay." or "I am sure you will do better when you do the cooking." My favorite is, "You were supposed to take me out to dinner. What happened to your promise?" I am grateful each time someone cooks for me. It means a few hours of rest which I appreciate.

3. Do not panic. Eliminate one or two dishes, if need be. Where does it say that you must have X amount of vegetables on the table, or an elaborate dessert when ice cream will do? Appetizers do not need to be present each time. If you had no time to prepare the zucchini with fresh tomato as you had planned, you just announce, "The zucchini looked so bad that I decided against it."
4. Never test a new recipe when guests are expected. First,

it saves embarrassment. Second, you won't have to feel like you failed. Third, this guest might be important. There is plenty of time to learn on your family in the privacy of your own sweet chosen time. Besides, it might be a future spouse you are trying to impress. Don't push it.

5. Prepare as much of it ahead of time as possible. So many items can be prepared ahead, and specialty grocery stores have a wonderful selection of salads, desserts, and breads for emergencies. Leave time to take a shower, comb your hair, and get dressed. Your guests will be most impressed by your relaxed manner and efficiency, and it will affect their enjoyment of the evening.

6. Don't be overzealous. Compensate with ready-made. From pizza to lasagna (at the gourmet counter in your reputable grocery store) to appetizing Greek salads, lemon chicken, and stuffed pork chops, the array amazes any hard-core gourmet.

7. If you are not good at decorating the table or dishes, don't worry. You can compensate with a low centerpiece or candles (not too high, so you can see your guests). Check the party store for ideas for table decorations. In fact, why not pick up a couple, just to be prepared for special events and holidays?

8. Go lightly with spices. Basic Rule: You can add spice, but there is no way you will be able to retrieve it, so have the hot stuff and extra Parmesan on a side table with only salt and pepper on the table.

The most important rule of them all is, "Always treat yourself!"

SURVIVAL TECHNIQUES AND THE UNEXPECTED GUEST

Let us look at the last minute dinner guest when the spouse phones from the office. "Honey, I have invited my boss over," or, "Sweetheart, an important client has just pulled into the city. I had no other choice but to invite him." Boy, does "Honey" or "Sweetheart" sting at this moment! Has this happened to you?

Coping with this situation is actually simple. Don't get angry. It won't help. Don't panic. Stay calm. Your response is, "Good, your honey will cook for you and your illustrious guest. On your way home, stop at the deli to pick up a palm salad (you name it), and/or stop at the bakery for bread and dessert ." Be specific and be firm.

"I don't have the time," is the usual reply.

There is no need to be conniving or vengeful. Just reply in your sweetest voice, "Honey, after all, it is your guest. I know you want the best for him or her." Your spouse will probably mutter something, so help out a little. Men, especially, need to have coaching in matters of entertaining. "Tell your guest, 'My wife has been very busy lately.' So we are going to stop and get a special salad (or whatever dish you decide). I tried it some time ago and it is delicious." The chances are your boss, client, or future prospect will admire your contribution to the evening and consideration for your spouse. Another explanation could be for your spouse: "I have tried a wine with a great bouquet. I am going to get a couple of bottles at the store. We will enjoy it with our dinner."

Now, you only have to cope with one dish for the main course and a couple of vegetables, which you can enhance from a can. Remember — you have been put on short notice, and it is not your fault. Dishes such as chicken breasts in blackberry sauce, pork chops with peach gravy, or fish in tarragon mustard sauce are easy to defrost and still take less than thirty minutes to prepare, leaving you time to set the table and shower. Don't forget that your spouse owes you an evening out on the town for being such a good sport.

SALT

Putting salt on beef is a debatable issue. Some chefs say it toughens the meat, and others argue that it does not make any difference. As for me, I put salt on all meat, from roast to steak, stewing beef, flank — it makes no difference to me. The age of the meat resting after the slaughter is vital. A period of 21 days is necessary to relax the muscle, which your grocery store or local butcher has already taken care of.

You will note that I have indicated "a dash or a pinch of salt to taste" quite often in the recipes included in the book. The reason for this is that so many of the ingredients already have salt included that you may want to allow your guests to add salt to the portions after they have tasted the food. This also covers your guests that maybe on a "salt restricted" diet.

COOKING STEAKS, PORK CHOPS, AND CHICKEN PIECES

I discovered a long time ago in my apprenticeship that dusting chicken pieces or cuts of meat with flour prior to cooking them in a frying pan seals the juice in. This practice includes all my steaks and pork chops since it keeps them juicy and tender. Please do not poke the meat. It dries out the meat and toughens it.

All-purpose flour is best, but if you don't have any go ahead and use what you have such as wheat, self-rising, unbleached, etc.

WHIPPING CREAM VS. DIET FOOD

It is also called 35% or heavy cream. The French use a lot of whipping cream in their recipes and don't get overweight. Sickening, isn't it? Well, it is because they balance the entire food chain every day of their lives with variety and the inclusion of the basic food groups.

Moderation is another factor. It could be that we would eat less if the foods we ingest are tasty and satisfying instead of bland and unfulfilling. The habit of eating on the run without even knowing what we have consumed as compared to sitting down to a table to enjoy a freshly prepared meal is another factor which contributes to our eating more and enjoying it less. So use whipping cream in moderation without guilt, and I think you will find that the additional taste will inspire you to eat smaller portions. Chew and Savor!

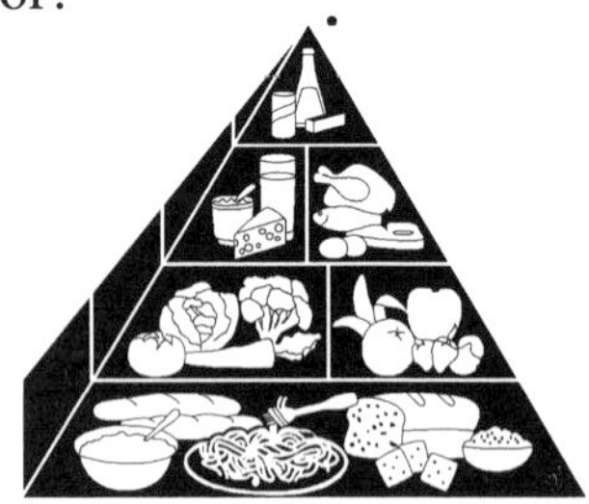

THE QUEEN

The whole city of Toronto heard about celebrating the sesquicentennial a whole two years in advance. Every radio station, newspaper, and TV station talked about it, made special programs and ran articles about what sort of festivities were going to be taking place. Of course, there was the standard parade, cleaning and stocking every park with fresh flowers, a display of fireworks, bands in the street, and dancing. The city came up with a wonderful twist, at least in my personal opinion. We (as the city of Toronto) were to greet the tall ships, nine of them in all, including two massive galleons and five proud standing mass frigates. All these ancient, shiny, renovated relics of the past were coming out of their resting hangars to salute us — from the mom-and-pop Torontonian, all the way to dignitaries such as the Prime Minister of Canada, the mayor of Toronto, and Her Majesty, the Queen of England. All the ships were to come together in full sail with all men on deck dressed in white. As a matter of fact, when it happened it was absolutely breathtaking. I was tired like I have never been before in my life; however, the sight of nine wooden ships in full sail gracefully gliding on Lake Ontario's blue water gave me immense joy, while waking me up in the process. "What does it have to do with cooking?" you may ask. Well, don't be so impatient. Read on.

I worked for a large restaurant and catering firm at the time. The General Manager walked in and asked us to give him our full attention. The *maitre d'* came to fetch us in the kitchen. Waiters, bus boys, dishwashers, salad people, and prep employees dropped everything to huddle in the dining room.

"Is everybody here?" he asked loudly.

"Yes," we answered as the silence followed. Anxiously we waited for the message he was about to deliver.

"Next week Her Majesty, the Queen of England, is coming to Toronto, if she can free herself from her royal obligations." A murmur ran through all the employees as he took a brief pause. "If she comes to Toronto, we have been chosen by the Prime Minister to do the banquet of honor."

"When will we know?" asked the *maitre d'*.

"In four days." The news hit us like a steam roller running through the restaurant dining room.

"You mean we will have three days to get ready."

"Yes."

"Do you anticipate many people at this event?" I asked.

"Twenty-seven hundred," he dropped calmly. "We will have the full spread: hot station, cold one, dessert, ice carving, all uniforms freshly starched. You will all have fifteen minutes to change before the service."

"What is the menu?"

"I will be informed in four days, which won't leave you much time for ordering the food, getting organized, preparation, and cooking."

For most employees, it meant overtime and perhaps a bonus. For the rest of us, the *maitre d'*, chefs, station managers, and head waiters, it was a challenge of magnitude we never even dreamed of. It would be a task we would carry in our hearts for years. Imagine us cooking for the epitome of the *creme de la creme* of Canada. Not the pretentious, the fake or wannabes — we were to prepare a feast for the pillars of the country we were so proud of. We all talked for four days, anxiously waiting for an answer from the General Manager. We walked tall, daydreaming while anticipating the challenge awaiting us around the corner. None of us got much sleep the next four days as tension mounted.

When the General Manager came to announce the good news of the arrival of Her Majesty the Queen of England, it spread through the restaurant, hitting us with the power of a tsunami and sweeping us off our feet.

We received an immediate notice to join the General Manager in his office to discuss the menu. It became a stampede to get the best seat, each of us ready with pen and paper. He gave each one of us a menu, together with the highlights of events and timing of services. In a job of this magnitude, timing is the key to success.

We asked our usual professional questions. There was no more time to fool around. Our minds were sharply focused on maybe the most prestigious job in our lives. *Maitre d's*, head waiters, and station managers went in one corner of the restaurant to prepare a plan of action. We chefs were in the other corner with the catering director dictating the menu, translating the quantities of food into cases, pounds, or gallons; what silverware and which plates were to be used; how many portable stoves per station; how many persons per table; how many tables, including prep, display, and guest tables; how many propane tanks; a tent for last minute preparation; a tent for the employees to change; and fridges to be transported. The list went on and on. It was an enormous task.

As for the menu, it was a doozie:

18,000 mini-shish kebabs

6,000 mini-wiener schnitzels

1400 pounds fresh asparagus

5 jumbo shrimp per person making a total of 13,500 pounds

9,000 small crepes (one with seafood, one with Beef Bourguignonne, one for dessert for each guest which I personally cooked during an eleven-hour shift working ten frying pans at a time).

The first item disturbed us — 18,000 mini-shish kebabs. "Why so many?" I asked the catering officer.

"We will give 12,000 complimentary kebabs to the Torontonians who will be trying to get a glimpse of the dignitaries." We skewered 18,000 kebabs. Imagine! We had slivers all over our fingers. Also, we lost count somewhere past 17,500, but we knew no one would double check.

It was a mind-boggling task with food everywhere. The fridges were loaded. We rented refrigerated trucks to store the overflow. What mattered in the end was that we did the job. Chefs, *maitre d's*, managers, and the General Manager were running around making sure every detail had been taken care of, that each particle of food was in place, and checking employee uniforms to insure their impeccable appearance.

Then the General Manager approached me. “François, you are on the shrimp station. You are serving the Queen.” My mouth dropped, and I stopped breathing for a second. “Who, me?” He answered, “Yes. Get ready.”

“I will never be ready, sir. I’ll be glad to, sir,” I babbled, confused, honored, scared, happy, panicked, surprised, amazed. I felt like I was floating six inches off the ground. I was in a frenzy.

“I am counting on you. Make the best of it.”

“Absolutely, sir.” I took off like a bullet to my station to make sure it was ready, checking each ingredient one hundred times in my head, taking out each wrinkle from the tablecloth with my own hand. I put on a newly starched chef hat. Everything was starched rigid to the point of hearing it crackling. No one could talk to me. I was drooling from joy, so proud that my career was at its peak. I put an ice cube on each of my temples to calm myself down, while butterflies in my stomach worked overtime. When Her Majesty, the Queen of England walked in with the Prime Minister and practically the entire house of Parliament, as well as a multitude of guests, I was ready. Our General Manager was walking amongst them, explaining each station and introducing specific Toronto guests.

When they arrived at my station, our General Manager said, “Here we cook *shrimp au pernod.”*

She looked at me, my frying pan and various ingredients and whispered softly, “Very nice.” She walked away. Is that it? One second? She didn’t have one comment! I felt like candle flame suddenly plunged into water. All my anticipation was snuffed away.

Oh, well. The job was done with flying colors. We each received a letter from the Office of the Prime Minister, and I got to see the tall ships, including the Blue Nose, the fastest frigate ever built. It is the ship forever engraved on the back of the Canadian dime. Whenever people ask me how the Queen was, I reply with a smile, “Very nice.”

Sauces, Gravies, Salad Dressings, And Salads

SAUCES

How many times have you ordered an entree and marveled over the exquisite taste of the sauce? Perhaps it was a basic cut of beef or a chicken breast, but the sauce made the dish to die for!

In this section you will find an array of easy-to-prepare sauces that will please your palate and delight your guests with your gourmet presentations. Just relax and let your creativity flow.

BASIC BROWN GRAVY OR DEMI GLACE

There are many sauces and gravies out there, all ranging in level of difficulty. Fortunately, this book will bypass the nearly impossible task of making gravy from scratch to get on with the pleasures of eating a delicious meal and leaving quality time to spend with friends and family.

You can go the old-fashioned way and cook up a stock with bones and vegetable condiments for twelve to twenty-four hours on the corner of the stove, then put it through a strainer and reduce it more for an additional four to eight hours, but never mind. Get the brown packaged sauce from the store (gravy from beef, chicken, or turkey). Your grocery store has your favorite brand. Simply follow the package directions for your basic brown gravy.

These sauces are so easy to make that even men can do it to impress their dates. Come on. Get creative!

VARIATIONS

Proceed with your regular brown gravy; then add one to two tablespoons of mustard to taste, and two teaspoons of chopped dill pickles. This is excellent on breaded pork chops. *(Charcutiere* Sauce)

You can add one or two ounces of whipping cream to the gravy, and it will be velvety.

Black or red currant, peach, black cherry, and raspberry sauces are all made the same way. Follow the instructions from your gravy package. Add between two and four teaspoons of your favorite jam. I go by taste and have a tendency to opt for 4 teaspoons. Bring to a boil and add two to three ounces of heavy cream. You have a whole variety of sauces from your leftover jars in the fridge. Fruit sauce goes well on pork, sweet sausage, duck, or chicken breasts. One of my favorites is fig sauce, from fig jam, which I use over duck.

You can also obtain a great red wine sauce by reducing 1½ cups of red wine to approximately ½ cup by simmering it over a low flame. Add the wine to a brown gravy. You can also add a liqueur like Porto, Grand Marnier, Sabra (a great substitute for Grand Marnier from Israel), or brandy to the brown gravy. Add it to the gravy sparingly (like a dash at a time, until it tastes good to you). Turn off the heat at first boil. Remember, alcohol evaporates when you cook it, so you won't get tipsy.

A L'ORANGE SAUCE (my discovery)

- ☐ 1 package brown gravy
- ☐ 4 teaspoons orange marmalade
- ☐ 1 ounce of Grand Marnier

Follow the instructions on the package to make the gravy. Add the orange marmalade and cook approximately one minute and add Grand Marnier. Whisk while adding a dab of cream (optional). You can substitute Cointro, Triple Sec, or Sabra (an orange liqueur from Israel) for the Grand Marnier. It's great on chicken and pork.

GREEN PEPPERCORN SAUCE

- ☐ 2 heaping tablespoons flour
- ☐ 2 beef bouillon cubes
- ☐ ½ onion, finely chopped
- ☐ 1 tablespoon oil
- ☐ ½ jar of green peppercorns in water (about 2 ounces; check your grocery store — it is not always easy to locate)
- ☐ ½ pint heavy cream (35% or whipping)
- ☐ ½ cup white wine

Put the the oil in a cooking pan. Add the chopped onion; sauté until it is almost clear. Add ½ cup of water and the ½ cup of wine. Bring it to a boil and add the beef cubes. Take out the green peppercorns; crush them with the bottom of a clean frying pan by applying pressure on the soft peppercorns. Mix four to five ounces of water into the flour with a whisk until all lumps disappear. (If you put the flour in the water, it will get lumpy; add water to flour, and it will get smooth.) Pour in the boiling broth gently while briskly whipping. Add the crushed peppercorns, then add the cream.

For more bite, add some of the juice from the peppercorns. It is good on New York steak or sautéed chicken breasts.

Always mix water into flour to avoid lumps in your sauce.

HOLLANDAISE SAUCE

This is a rather difficult, temperamental sauce to make from scratch, so my advice is to use a package from your grocery store and follow the instructions. You can get creative by adding different ingredients to vary the flavor. Blend in a teaspoon of caviar or tomato paste during cooking. A dab of fresh cream will lighten it up for your fresh asparagus. Adding a touch of dill or cayenne pepper, or even a little grated horseradish or curry, can spice up your sauce for variety.

Enjoy Hollandaise sauce on asparagus, fish, and all vegetables. It tastes good no matter what.

BEARNAISE SAUCE

It is the same as Hollandaise sauce — a moody proposition. This sauce has a tendency to separate, and it is impossible to get it back when making it from scratch. So don't worry. Use a package from your grocery story and follow the instructions.

BOLOGNESE SAUCE (Meat Sauce)

- ☐ 1 pound ground beef
- ☐ 1 teaspoon thyme
- ☐ ½ onion, chopped
- ☐ 3 garlic cloves, chopped
- ☐ 1 can tomato sauce (8 or 15 ounce)
- ☐ 8 ounces sliced mushrooms (optional)
- ☐ 1 green pepper, chopped (optional)
- ☐ 1 to 2 tablespoons olive oil, or your favorite oil
- ☐ Salt and pepper to taste

Put the ground beef in a pan. Add 1 cup water; mix well. Bring the meat and water to a boil. As soon as it starts boiling, mix one more time with a wooden spoon. Drain the water, fat and all liquids through a colander. Gently rinse meat in cold water. Wipe the pan with a paper towel. Put the pan back on the stove with the oil, chopped onions, green peppers (optional), thyme, and mushrooms (optional). Sauté 3 to 5 minutes. Add the garlic, can of tomato sauce, meat from the colander, salt, and pepper, and simmer for 5 minutes. *Bon appetit*!

If you want, you can add oregano, Tabasco, basil, capers, more garlic, olives, or Italian seasoning to taste — just one at a time, please. For a change, try replacing the ground beef with leftover chopped turkey or ham, but do not cook the meat or rinse.

First cook the onions, thyme, and mushrooms in the oil; after 5 minutes of cooking, add the chopped ham or turkey, tomato, garlic, etc. Simmer to take away the bitterness of the tomato and add one pinch of sugar. One pinch, Darling — not ¼ spoon, just a tiny bit.

CHEESE SAUCE

- ☐ 1 pint milk, regular or skim
- ☐ 2 tablespoons all-purpose flour
- ☐ 2 tablespoons butter
- ☐ 8 ounces cheese, shredded or grated (your choice of yellow, white or even blue cheese)

Warm up the milk in a cooking pan. Pay attention — it boils over easily. In another pan melt the butter. Add the flour to the butter with a whisk at low heat.

Now pour the hot milk into the pan containing the butter and flour. Put the flame back at medium heat and whisk until smooth. Add the cheese and stir one minute while cooking, and then take it off the stove.

This is good over broccoli, cauliflower, and macaroni and cheese. For *nachos*, just add cayenne pepper, jalapenos, and olives, and this becomes a hot cheese dip. It is called "dressed up." For a vegetable dip, use blue cheese for the cheese.

> If the sauce is too thick, depending on your choice of cheeses, a couple of ounces of milk while boiling will loosen it up.

TZAZIKI SAUCE (Greek Cucumber Garlic Sauce)

- ☐ 4 cucumbers, peeled and seeded
- ☐ 4 garlic cloves (add 1 or 2 more, if you love garlic like I do!)
- ☐ ¼ teaspoon curry
- ☐ 8 ounces low-fat or no-fat sour cream
- ☐ A dash Worcestershire sauce to taste
- ☐ Salt to taste

Dice the peeled and seeded cucumber, and place in a colander. Sprinkle with salt and toss it. Sprinkle again. Do this three times. Let it sit in the sink for one hour. (The salt will draw out the liquid.) Peel and chop the garlic. Put the cucumber in a blender and blend until smooth. Put a paper towel in the bottom of the colander and pour the cucumber in it; let it drain for 10 minutes.

Put the sour cream, curry, Worcestershire sauce, and garlic into a blender and mix. Then pour into a large bowl. Blend in the cucumber thoroughly with a whisk. Chill for one hour. It tastes good with grilled meat, fish, and as a sauce for your homemade hamburger. It is excellent as a dip with fresh vegetables. You will have all your friends asking you for the recipe.

TOMATO-MUSHROOM SAUCE

- ☐ 1 can tomato sauce (8 or 15 ounce, your choice)
- ☐ 1 pound mushrooms
- ☐ 1 small onion, chopped
- ☐ ½ tablespoon thyme
- ☐ 2 bay leaves
- ☐ 1 tablespoon olive oil (it is better)
- ☐ 4 to 5 cloves garlic (if you are like me, make it 10 since I love the stuff)

Chop the onion. Slice the mushrooms. (You probably have bought the sliced ones at your store. Well, good for you. You deserve the break.) Put a pan on the stove at medium heat; add the oil. Now add the onion, bay leaves, and thyme. Cook for 2 minutes. (Make it 3 or 4. I promise I won't tell.) Add the mushrooms; mix well. Put it at low heat. Add the garlic and cover with a lid. Cook 10 minutes or so; then, add the tomato sauce and simmer another 5 minutes. Now it is ready to serve, so take out the bay leaves. Turn off the range. Sit down and relax. Have your hubby serve you this delectable sauce with linguini. You deserve to sit down; you cooked it!

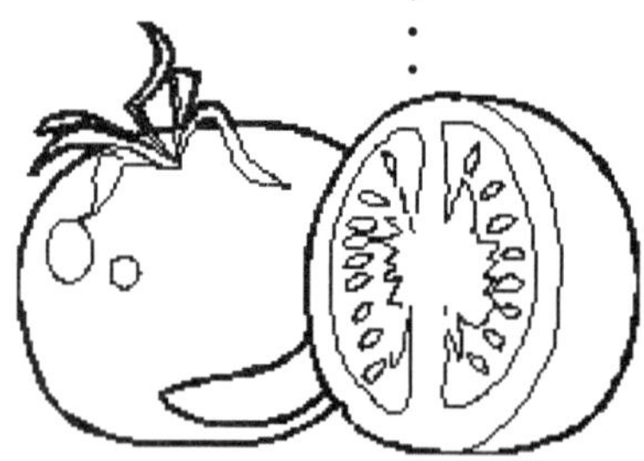

FRESH TOMATO-MUSHROOM SAUCE

- ☐ 4 to 5 fresh, ripe, large tomatoes
- ☐ 1 pound mushrooms (pre-sliced, if you wish)
- ☐ 1 small onion
- ☐ ½ teaspoon thyme
- ☐ ¼ teaspoon oregano
- ☐ 1 chicken bouillon cube dissolved in 4 ounces water
- ☐ 4 to 5 garlic cloves
- ☐ 1 tablespoon olive oil (or other will do)
- ☐ Ground pepper (fresh is better) to taste
- ☐ Salt to taste

Chop the onion. Cut the tomato in small pieces (don't be too precise — I won't scold you). Slice the mushrooms. Peel and chop the garlic. Now we are ready.

In a pan put the oil, onion, oregano, and thyme. Cook until the onions are soft. Add the mushrooms and sauté an additional 5 minutes. Add the garlic and tomato; mix well. Add the chicken bouillon cube and a pinch of salt. Simmer covered for 10 to 12 minutes at low heat. Mix one more time. Serve hot over pasta, baked chicken breast, pork chops, or chopped steak.

THE CAKE

I worked for an exclusive club nestled between twin towers on the shore of Lake Ontario, right on the Toronto City limits. A ceiling of glass made the two edifices look even more dramatic. On top of the forty-sixth floor, the clubhouse reserved exclusively for the condominium owners overlooked the Toronto skyline. On any evening the sunset gave a display no one could describe in words. The water of Lake Ontario stretched as far as the eye could see, reflecting the last glimmers of the sun's rays.

I went often to the top of the tower in the club for contemplation. Anniversaries, bachelor parties, and weddings were frequent occurrences there, and I was the one to call for coordinating events. We did a wedding for 178 people including the preparation. The napkins, skirting, and table cloths, as well as silverware, glasses, and all the food and drinks had to be transported each time. We only had a warm-up kitchen, a holding area and one prep table for last minute touch ups.

We were frantically preparing for this wonderful occasion taking place on a Saturday afternoon. At one p.m. Lex approached me. "Hey Chef. What time is the cake coming?"

"It should have been here by eleven a.m."

"Well, it is one p.m. and no one is here."

"Give me a minute. I'll call them." I headed for the kitchen office, picked up the phone and called the bakery. It took approximately fifteen rings to get a soul to answer.

"Hola que tal." Fortunately, I speak the lingo, so I asked him in Spanish to give me the man in charge. "There is no one here. We close at noon on Saturday."

"How long are you going to be there?"

"Thirty more minutes," he replied.

"I'll be right over to pick up the cake for Stephanie's 178 people."

"You can't. All the fridges are locked."

"Good. That creates a dilemma. Well, you have a nice

day." I hung up, still not sure of what to do. My brother was out of town. I had no capacity to bake a cake and cool it off in two hours.

What about Patric! Why not? He is the best baker in Toronto. He is the funniest Frenchman I ever met, with two apprenticeships to his credentials. He is a master party chef and a *chef de cuisine.* He would probably laugh at me, but ultimately he would know what to do. I located his number in minutes. Whenever I called him, I always knew his answer, *"Oui, allo."*

"Patric? François. I need a cake."

"For when?"

"Right now. 178 people."

"Okay, *Toto.* I am coming. Prepare the coffee. Any special flavor?"

"Yes. Chocolate."

"Give me one hour. I'll be there."

He hung up without asking if anything needed to be written on the cake or about the color scheme. He did not seem worried. Well, I wasn't either, having other pressing problems at hand. It took only fifty-five minutes for Patric to show up. His dishwasher was driving the van with the air conditioning at full tilt. Patric was in the back decorating a slab of chocolate cake. He was sitting on the metal wheel well, a piping bag in his hand. I opened the door.

"Alor, Toto. Any particular writing? I made you a chocolate orange cake." The wedding was a success. We pulled off the gig at the last minute. I used Patric on many occasions after this incident, although I never thanked him enough for his effort. He saved the day from behind the scene.

SALAD DRESSINGS AND SALADS

Dressings are easy, so let's start with the basics. Vinaigrettes are the fastest to do. Use a clean, airtight container. I prefer glass so that I can see what is in it. Using the oil you prefer, fill the container one-third full. To this, add approximately half this amount of vinegar (basic white or red wine vinegar) so that the container is now slightly over half full. Add a pinch of salt, a dash of Worcestershire sauce, and only a pinch of black or white pepper. Close the lid tightly and shake well. There you have it — a basic vinaigrette.

Now that you mastered this basic salad enhancer, let's have fun. It is the same recipe, but this time add one to two teaspoons of your favorite mustard. Again close the lid and shake well.

From now on, the process will be the same. Fill up your container but leave room to shake the ingredients, and be sure to close the lid.

VARIATIONS

Explore your kitchen cabinet to enhance your dressing. Try one or two teaspoons of one of the following for variety:

- ☑ add tarragon
- ☑ add parsley, fresh or dried
- ☑ add basil
- ☑ add chives or green onions
- ☑ add Italian seasoning
- ☑ add oregano
- ☑ add chopped onions and/or garlic
- ☑ add chopped pickles
- ☑ add chopped crab meat
- ☑ add chopped hard-boiled eggs
- ☑ add anchovy fillets

☑ add Parmesan cheese
☑ add chopped capers

Look through your cabinets and refrigerator. A dash of hickory smoke barbeque sauce, cayenne pepper, lemon or lime juice will give it zing. Remember to twist the lid tight and shake. You will have a new dressing each time. **Remember: Creation is the fun part of cooking.**

Let's now explore the possibility of Specialized Vinegars. Here are the simple rules. You must remember to substitute water for half of the vinegar. This is necessary to reduce the overwhelming potency of specialized vinegar. For example, in volume now you have 1 cup oil, ¼ cup vinegar, and ¼ cup water instead of 1 cup oil and ½ cup vinegar. Add the salt, pepper, and Worcestershire sauce (to taste); close the lid, and shake well. This is the base. Add whatever ingredients you fancy, from your favorite mustard to tarragon, chopped crab meat, parsley, basil, raspberries, Bing cherries, etc.

Some of the vinegars which will enhance your culinary effort are raspberry, strawberry, malt, cider, balsamic vinegars, or plain lemon juice will do. One of my favorites is Japanese rice vinegar. It is outstanding. Also experiment with an array of walnut, olive, grape seed or canola oils.

If your dressing gets too tart, a pinch of sugar or Sweet and Low (only a pinch), or a dash of water and oil will rectify the potent taste. Salads are usually tasteless and bland, so tasting the dressing from the jar with your finger (see, I know about your habits!) or spoon does not reflect the true taste. Instead take a salad leaf. Dip it in and drain the excess dressing. You will have a better idea of the flavor when you taste it this way.

Now, let's get on to the next fun project — a dressing with a mayonnaise base.

MAYONNAISE

- ☐ 1 pint (16 ounces) oil, vegetable or canola
- ☐ 5 egg yolks
- ☐ 1 tablespoon mustard, prepared or Dijon
- ☐ A pinch white pepper to taste
- ☐ Juice of one lemon or 1 tablespoon of plain white vinegar
- ☐ A dash Worcestershire sauce to taste (optional)
- ☐ A pinch of salt to taste

Place five egg yolks and one tablespoon of mustard in a bowl — prepared or Dijon will do, whichever you prefer. (I personally don't like the deep yellow one; it makes the mayonnaise look funny.) Add a pinch of salt, a pinch of white pepper (not black), and a dash of Worcestershire (optional) and either 1 ounce of plain white vinegar or the juice of one lemon (no seeds).

Blend for approximately two minutes with an electric mixer. It will start foaming. Don't stop the beater, which must be at full speed, except if you have one of those 15,000 RPM "on-steroids" type of electric gizmos. (Get the picture?) Beat it fast as you slowly add 1 pint of oil—first, a thin stream, and gradually increasing. When all the oil has become solid into a nice smooth mayonnaise, blend for 15 to 30 seconds more. It will firm up. This is your perfect homemade base for sandwiches, dressings, dips of all sorts, or simply for the burger you have been meaning to sink your teeth into.

CHANTILLY SAUCE

Add two tablespoons heavy whipping cream for each 1¼ cups of mayonnaise (good on freshly cooked asparagus); for a dip, just add cayenne pepper, just a little at a time to taste.

HORSERADISH SAUCE

Add horseradish to taste; add a small amount about one teaspoon to one cup of mayonaisse to start, because you can't remove it later if it's too much. It is good for cold fish, cold roast, beef sandwiches, or leftover prime rib. Add chopped walnuts for a great garnish.

REMOULADE SAUCE

- ☐ 2 tablespoons mustard
- ☐ 1 tablespoon chopped dill pickles (I prefer the shrub pickle because of the firmness, but a hard dill or Kosher will do.)
- ☐ ½ tablespoon chopped capers
- ☐ 2 chopped anchovies
- ☐ A pinch chopped parsley to taste
- ☐ A pinch chopped tarragon to taste

None of the ingredients are of absolute necessity, so lighten up. If you don't have some of them, don't worry. Forget them. Mix the ingredients that you do have with ½ cup mayonnaise. Great dip or sauce for fish!

SWEDISH SAUCE

- ☐ 1½ cups mayonnaise
- ☐ ½ cup applesauce
- ☐ 1 teaspoon mustard
- ☐ 1 teaspoon grated horseradish

Mix the ingredients thoroughly. This is excellent on pork chops, either fresh from the grill or leftover, cold roast pork, and even on leftover cold turkey; it is a change from the eternal cranberry sauce.

TARTAR SAUCE

- ☐ 2 hard-boiled eggs, chopped
- ☐ 2 teaspoons chopped pickles (dill or Kosher) Add more if you like
- ☐ 1 teaspoon chopped capers, but again add more if you like
- ☐ Chopped chives to taste (optional)
- ☐ Tabasco (Here again, it is up to you. Start with just a dash unless you like to melt the wax in your ears.)

Blend the ingredients with 1 cup mayonnaise and serve with fish.

GREEN SAUCE

Here is one for the hard-core Irish fanatic.

- ☐ 2 ounces spinach
- ☐ 2 ounces water chestnuts
- ☐ 1 heaping tablespoon tarragon
- ☐ 1 heaping tablespoon chervil
- ☐ A dash Worcestershire sauce or Tabasco to taste

Boil spinach, water chestnuts, tarragon, and chervil for 3 to 4 minutes; drain and rinse in cold water. Press between your hands to remove the excess water. Chop in a kitchen blender. Add to 1½ cup mayo. Add Worcestershire sauce or a dash of Tabasco. It is a great dip and can also be served with fish.

HUMUS

This is for vegetarians who are tired of bland food.

- ☐ 4 to 6 garlic cloves, peeled and chopped
- ☐ 2 cans chick peas
- ☐ 2 teaspoons tahini (Japanese specially ground sesame seed)
- ☐ A dash Worcestershire sauce to taste
- ☐ A dash cayenne pepper to taste
- ☐ Salt to taste

Drain the chickpeas, saving the liquid. Blend them until smooth, like a paste. Put the chickpeas in a bowl with the tahini, garlic, cayenne, Worcestershire, and a pinch of salt. Blend well with a whisk until smooth. If the humus seems too thick, thin it with some of the chick pea liquid. Humus is good on pita bread, and as a dip for vegetables. It is a nice late snack over fresh warm toast. *Bon appetit*!

NICOISE SALAD (Serves 4)

- ☐ 3 large potatoes cut into 1-inch cubes (approximately)
- ☐ 2 cans whole green beans, drained
- ☐ 2 cans solid tuna, drained
- ☐ ½ cup olive oil
- ☐ ¼ cup white vinegar
- ☐ 2 eggs
- ☐ 2 large ripe tomatoes cut into 1-inch cubes
- ☐ Black olives, as many as you want
- ☐ Salt to taste

Cook the potatoes in water on slow heat until soft but still together (approximately 10 to 12 minutes). Drain in a colander. Cook the eggs in boiling water 7 to 8 minutes, until hard, and cool off. Put the potatoes, drained green beans, drained tuna, and tomatoes in a bowl and mix gently. Add vinegar (to taste, approximately ¼ cup), olive oil (to taste also, approximately ½ cup), and a pinch of salt and mix again. Put the whole mixture in a clean bowl and decorate with the black olives (as many as you want) and the hard-boiled egg, cut into quarters or eighths. It's great for a summer main course.

THE GRADUATION PARTY

Many moons ago when I was in my late twenties I was sent to one of the most prestigious colleges in Canada to orchestrate the graduation party. I was to meet one other chef, a fine craftsman from Germany. We had to do the decoration, ice carving, salmon design, and Chaud Froid platter while the local chef had to cook the actual main dinner.

Like every year, they were expecting 1,500 people. It was to be done with no expenses spared, reflecting the few privileged elite people in this world. It was going to be a dazzling display of luscious food tantalizing every palate. By the presentation alone, the challenge for Eric and me was not only to impress the guests, but rather to push ourselves to our highest culinary expertise and beyond for the sheer pleasure of creating our own masterpieces.

We carved ice, making a dragon out of five blocks of ice. We hollowed out the center of pineapples by taking out the cores, drove a broomstick through each one to stack them up, and put a fresh fern on top to make them look like palm trees. We made a windmill out of nougadine (caramel sugar with crushed nuts).

We cooked a turkey, a capon (an extremely large chicken), and four regular chickens, roasted until golden brown. We stood them up with coat hangers, carved heads for them out of potatoes, and made drums out of turnips. In short, we made a musical band out of a half dozen roasted birds.

Whether we got noticed was irrelevant. We were so proud of our profession, and it wasn't often that we had carte blanche, without budget restrictions to worry about. We decorated lobsters and even ordered a dozen langoustes (also called rock lobsters) weighing at least five pounds each.

Eric and I were in a creative frenzy, working 18 hours a day without noticing the time, driven by an artist's adrenaline making one lose contact with the real world. It was sheer ecstasy complementing each other while the first guests entered the dining room. Not a single dish was out of place. Platters glistened with fresh fruit; the odors of freshly prepared hot dishes tickled everyone's noses. We had swapped our uniforms for fresh ones, starched and ironed, the noose perfectly tied on our chef necktie, and even our pants were ironed and our shoes waxed.

Naturally the male guests were wearing tuxedos while the ladies in their evening dresses looked distinguished and elegant. Eric and I walked up and down in back of the buffet to supervise the local cooking crew. Our job was basically finished. We were proud of our works of art and decided to stick around, mostly to look at the beautiful people.

We stood with our hands behind our backs, stiff like ironing boards in front of the cold section of the buffet. A gentleman showed a platter of our funny orchestra to one of his colleagues and asked politely, "How did they make this chicken stand up?" At that exact moment a lady in the same line, the second person behind the gentleman asking about the orchestra, swung back to look behind. She had apparently forgotten something, so she asked the person behind her in line to please hand her one of the delicacies on display. This left a very distinguished older lady in front of us looking at the penguins we had made out of hard-boiled eggs with black olives and carrots as the feet and beak, standing on a Styrofoam iceberg. She found it so irresistible she had to have one. As she bent forward and reached out to take it, one of her breasts fell out.

I was stunned by the unfortunate mishap, but not quite as surprised as she was, holding her plate with one hand while taking the darling penguin between her thumb and finger while her breast decided to go on an exploring expedition. Eric grabbed a serving spoon with his right hand, hooked her dress with his index finger and, while reaching over the table, scooped her wandering breast and put it back in place while apologizing to her.

"Allow me, Madam," he said without a smile. His face looked like a butler who had served the same family for fifty years. We both bowed to the lady.

The gentleman in the tux in front of her turned around and said to her, "You've got to see this orchestra made out of roasted chickens." We walked back to the kitchen, fell in the floor with laughter and rolled on the floor in our clean uniforms. We could not hold our laughter any longer. Basic Rule: Be prepared for the unexpected and keep a sense of humor!

Soups

SOUPS

For the novice, some of the easiest creations are soups. They can be prepared ahead of time either for your own nourishment after a hard day at work or for the enjoyment of your guests for an impromptu dinner on a chilly, autumn night. Throw together a salad or platter of fresh vegetables or fruits with one of your gourmet sauces. Pick up a loaf of French bread at the bakery, flowers and/or candles for the table and *Et voila* — **IT'S A SPECIAL OCCASION, AND YOU ARE THE STAR!**

How about a trim-the-tree party in December? Keep it simple. Have the soup simmering on the stove when your guests arrive. Hang a piece of mistletoe over the stove so that the cook and helpers are targets of affection as they work in the kitchen.

BOSTON CLAM CHOWDER

- ☐ 2 pounds potatoes, cleaned, peeled, and diced small (do not wash the potatoes after peeling)
- ☐ 1 large onion, chopped
- ☐ 4 to 6 stalks celery, cleaned and chopped
- ☐ 1 teaspoon thyme
- ☐ 2 bay leaves
- ☐ ½ pint cream
- ☐ 3 heaping tablespoons all-purpose flour
- ☐ 4 chicken bouillon cubes
- ☐ 1 tablespoon oil
- ☐ 4 cans baby clams
- ☐ A dash Worcestershire sauce to taste
- ☐ Salt to taste

In a large soup pan put the oil, onion, celery, bay leaves, and thyme. Cook until onions are soft. Add the juice from the clams, but not the clams. Add 5 cups water and the chicken bouillon cubes; cook for 15 minutes. Add the potatoes and simmer for 30 minutes. Gradually add approximately 6 ounces water to the flour by adding a little water to the flour, mixing it smooth, and then adding more water. Then whisk the flour and water mixture into the soup. Cook for a couple of minutes while stirring. Add the cream; add the clams. Add the salt and Worcestershire, if you like. Serve hot.

For **MANHATTAN CLAM CHOWDER**, proceed the same but when you add the potatoes, add also 1 can tomato sauce (6 to 8 ounces)

You can also use mushrooms with the celery, or chopped parsley for color when you blend in the cream.

A touch of curry will give your Boston or Manhattan clam chowder an interesting twist.

Always mix the water into the flour (not flour into water) to get a smooth consistency.

CREAM OF ASPARAGUS SOUP

- ☐ 2 bunches of fresh asparagus (about 1½ to 2 pounds), washed and drained
- ☐ 3 heaping tablespoons all-purpose flour
- ☐ ½ pint whipping cream
- ☐ A dash of salt to taste
- ☐ A dash Worcestershire sauce to taste

Bring 1 quart of water to a boil; when boiling, add the asparagus and cook uncovered for 5 minutes. Remove the asparagus with tongs and add 2 chicken bouillon cubes and a dash of Worcestershire sauce to the water on the stove. Cool off the asparagus and then remove and discard the lower third of the stalk. Cut the remaining asparagus into 1 inch pieces (approximately).

Gradually mix 5 ounces of water into three heaping tablespoons of all-purpose flour and blend until all the lumps are gone. If the mixture is too thick, gently add a bit more water. Pour in the boiling broth while whisking; it will thicken quickly. Add ½ pint of whipping cream, also called 35% or heavy cream. Toss in the pieces of asparagus; add salt, if necessary. There it is; it's that simple.

The flour will react differently based on the humidity and altitude of your area. If the soup is too thin, add more mixture of cold water and flour, blending it slowly into the soup while it simmers. You can chop ½ can of red sweet peppers for garnish.

NOTE : Do not salt the water prior to cooking the asparagus. Add the salt afterwards.

A chef's secret or shortcut: Peel the onion removing as little as possible from the root. Cut the onion in half lengthwise from the root to the stem. Put the flat side on the cutting board with the root away from you. With the stem toward you make 10 to 15 incisions all the way down to the cutting board, but only 3/4 through the root. Give your onion a half turn and cut again. The root of your onion will hold the layers together. *Et Voila*, you have a professionally chopped onion!

To simply slice the onion, put the flat side on the cutting board and slice across the onion from the stem moving toward the root.

ONION SOUP (Serves 4)

- ☐ 6 large sliced onions
- ☐ 4 beef bouillon cubes
- ☐ 2 cloves garlic, peeled and chopped
- ☐ 1 pinch thyme
- ☐ 2 tablespoons oil (your choice, but no olive oil, please)
- ☐ 4 cups water

Peel the onions and cut in half. Slice the onions and put them into a large cooking pan with the oil. Cook at high temperature. Stir often until the onion juice evaporates. You will know because the bottom will slowly turn brown. Add 4 cups of water; add the thyme, beef cubes, and garlic. When it starts boiling, lower the temperature and simmer 20 minutes. Add salt to taste, if necessary.

Substituting one cup of white wine for one of the cups of water will enhance the taste of the onion soup. Remember, the wine is optional.

FRENCH ONION SOUP

- ☐ 6 large sliced onions
- ☐ 4 beef bouillon cubes
- ☐ 2 cloves garlic, peeled and chopped
- ☐ 1 pinch thyme
- ☐ 2 tablespoons oil (your choice, but no olive oil, please)
- ☐ 3 cups water
- ☐ 1 cup white wine
- ☐ Grated cheese, Monterey Jack or mozzarella (I prefer Gruyere which has a much stronger taste.)
- ☐ Croutons or toasted bread to taste

Proceed the same as for onion soup. Substitute 1 cup of wine for one of the cups of water. When the soup is in the bowl or soup plate, gently place the croutons or toasted bread on top. Sprinkle with the cheese. Serve hot. The French call it *gratinee* when it is melted under a broiler.

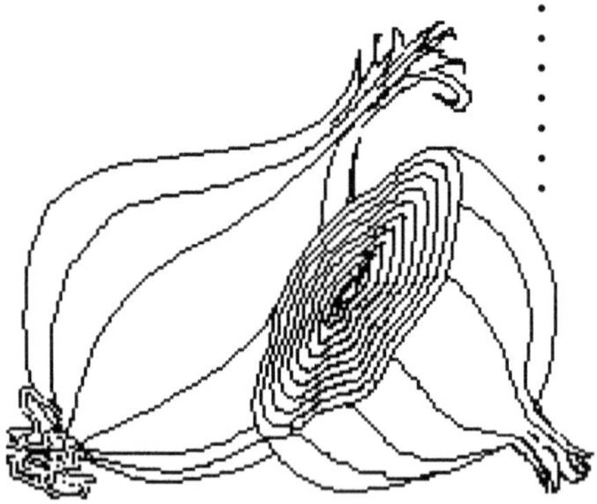

VICHYSSOISE

- ☐ 2 pounds potatoes, diced (don't wash them after dicing)
- ☐ 2 pounds white leeks, sliced and well washed (don't use too much of the green top)
- ☐ 1 onion
- ☐ 3 chicken bouillon cubes
- ☐ ½ pint whipping cream (35%)
- ☐ 1 tablespoon oil
- ☐ Fresh or dried chives to taste
- ☐ A dash Worcestershire sauce to taste

Sauté the onion and leeks in a pan until soft. Add 4 cups water, the chicken cubes, and 1 or 2 dashes Worcestershire sauce. Cook for about 10 minutes. Add the diced potatoes. (Do not wash, rinse, or store the potatoes when diced; it will wash off the starch, interfering with the binding.) Cook covered for 1 hour at low heat; then turn it off and let it cool for 1 hour or more.

When it is cold enough to handle, blend until it becomes a smooth paste. Put it in a container in the fridge for 4 to 6 hours. When chilled, blend in the cream. Serve with the chives as a decoration.

MUSSEL SOUP (Serves 4)

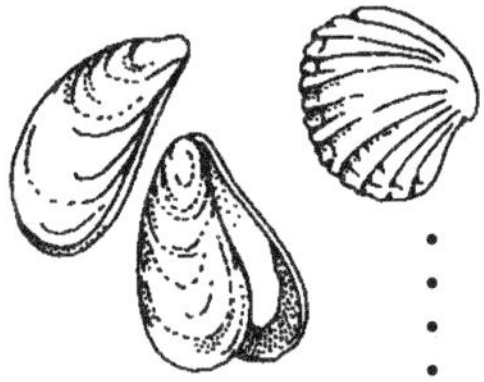

- ☐ 4 pounds clean mussels
- ☐ 1 large chopped onion
- ☐ ¼ teaspoon thyme
- ☐ 2 garlic cloves
- ☐ 1 tablespoon olive oil
- ☐ ½ pint cream
- ☐ 2 chicken bouillon cubes
- ☐ 1 cup white wine
- ☐ 2 heaping tablespoons all-purpose flour
- ☐ Salt and pepper to taste
- ☐ A dash Worcestershire sauce to taste

Sauté the onion and thyme in oil until the onions are soft. Add the freshly rinsed mussels with 1 cup white wine and the garlic. Bring to a boil and mix thoroughly. Put a lid on and cook for 1 minute. Turn off the heat but do not remove the lid. Cool off for 30 minutes to 1 hour. Remove the lid and take the mussels out of the broth, one by one. Keep the broth. Separate the mussels from their shells and discard the shell.

WARNING : The mussels that are tightly closed must be discarded.

The pan with the liquid, onions, garlic, and thyme goes back on the burner with 4 cups of water*. Bring it to a boil and simmer for 10 to 15 minutes. Mix the flour with approximately 4 ounces of cold water until smooth (always mix the water into the flour, not flour into water). Pour it into the boiling broth while whisking. Add salt, pepper, and Worcestershire sauce to taste. Add the cream when it starts boiling, and it is ready.

Put the mussels into the broth at the last minute, after the cream starts boiling. They will stay soft. Or, you can put 6 to 8 mussels in each plate or soup cup, and pour the hot soup on top of it. For decoration you can sprinkle chopped parsley or chopped chives or paprika on top of each bowl of soup before serving.

* For a holiday treat, add a pinch of dried saffron with the 4 cups of water when you start cooking the broth.

CREAM OF CAULIFLOWER SOUP (Serves 4)

- ☐ 1 whole large cauliflower (broken in pieces, with core discarded, or a pre-cleaned package)
- ☐ 1 onion, chopped
- ☐ 2 heaping tablespoons flour
- ☐ ½ pint cream
- ☐ 2 chicken bouillon cubes
- ☐ 1 bay leaf
- ☐ Amino acid to taste (pg. 96)
- ☐ Salt to taste

Put 4 cups water in a pan together with the onion. Bring it to a boil; then reduce the heat and add the cauliflower, 2 bouillon cubes, and bay leaf. Simmer covered for 20 to 30 minutes. Mix the 4 ounces water into the 2 heaping tablespoons flour. Whisk the flour and water mixture into the soup. Don't stop whisking to prevent lumps. In the process, it will break the cauliflower. This is good. When it starts boiling again, add the cream and whisk one more time. Add amino acid and salt to taste.

OPTION: To enhance your cauliflower soup, you can put in 3 to 4 ounces blue cheese at the last minute while adding the cream.

CREAM OF MUSHROOM SOUP (Serves 4)

- ☐ 1 large onion, chopped
- ☐ 1 pound sliced mushrooms (pre-sliced will do)
- ☐ 1 bay leaf
- ☐ ½ teaspoon thyme
- ☐ ½ tablespoon amino acid (pg. 96)
- ☐ 1 tablespoon butter or oil
- ☐ ½ pint whipping cream (35%)
- ☐ 2 heaping tablespoons flour
- ☐ A dash Worcestershire sauce to taste
- ☐ Salt to taste

Put the butter or oil in a pan with the onions, thyme and bay leaf. Sauté until the onions get soft. Add the mushrooms and keep cooking until they get soft. Add 3 cups water and bring to a boil; then lower the heat and add the amino acid. Simmer for 15 minutes. Mix the 4 ounces water into the flour. Pour the mixture of flour and water into the soup while whisking. When it starts to boil again, add the cream. Add salt, if necessary. Remove the bay leaves before serving.

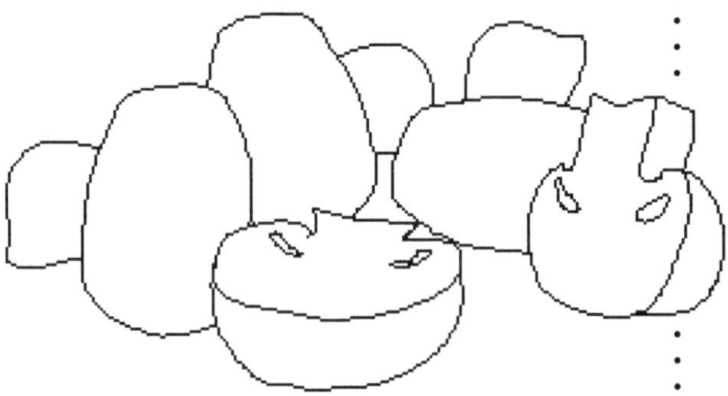

LEEK-TOMATO SOUP (Serves 4)

- ☐ 1 small onion
- ☐ 1 bunch leeks (about 1 to 1¼ pound), cleaned and chopped
- ☐ ¼ teaspoon thyme
- ☐ 1 can plain tomato sauce (4 to 8 ounces)
- ☐ 3 chicken bouillon cubes
- ☐ 1 to 2 heaping tablespoons all-purpose flour
- ☐ 1 tablespoon oil or butter
- ☐ 1 cup whipping cream
- ☐ A dash Worcestershire sauce to taste
- ☐ Salt to taste

Put the chopped leeks in a large container with water. All the particles of sand will go to the bottom while the leeks float to the top. Slice or chop the onion. Relax; it doesn't matter. Put the oil or butter (whichever you fancy) in a pan together with the onion. Cook until soft. Pick the leeks gently out of the water and add to the pan with the onions and butter. Add the thyme and cook for 5 more minutes. Add 3 cups of water, the bouillon cubes, a pinch of salt, and a dash of Worcestershire sauce. Mix thoroughly. Wait until it starts boiling and add the can of plain tomato sauce. Simmer for 15 minutes at medium heat. Mix 1 cup of water into the flour until smooth, and then whisk it slowly into the simmering soup. Add a cup of fresh whipping cream after you have thickened it with the flour, but before turning the heat off. It will make your soup a divine delicacy. Serve whenever you are ready.

MUSHROOM-TOMATO SOUP (Serves 4)

- ☐ 1 small onion
- ☐ 1 to 1½ pounds mushrooms (depending on your taste for mushrooms)
- ☐ 1 can plain tomato sauce (your choice, 4 to 8 ounces)
- ☐ 3 chicken bouillon cubes
- ☐ 1 to 2 heaping tablespoons all-purpose flour
- ☐ 1 tablespoon oil or butter
- ☐ ¼ teaspoon thyme
- ☐ 1 bay leaf
- ☐ ½ pint 35% cream
- ☐ 2 garlic cloves
- ☐ A dash Worcestershire sauce to taste
- ☐ Salt to taste

Slice or chop the onion; slice the mushrooms. Put the oil in a pan on the stove at medium heat. Add the onion, thyme and bay leaf; cook until the onion gets soft. Add the mushrooms and cook for another 2 to 3 minutes. Add the chopped garlic and 3 cups water. Bring it all to a boil. Add the chicken cubes, a pinch salt, and 2 dashes Worcestershire sauce and cook for 15 minutes. Add the can of tomato sauce and boil 5 more minutes. Gradually mix the water into the flour (approximately 1 cup water for 2 heaping tablespoons flour). Whisk well until no lumps are remaining. Pour slowly into the broth until it thickens (not too thick — we don't want to make glue for wallpaper). Add the cream. Take it off the stove as soon as it boils. Remove the bay leaf before serving.

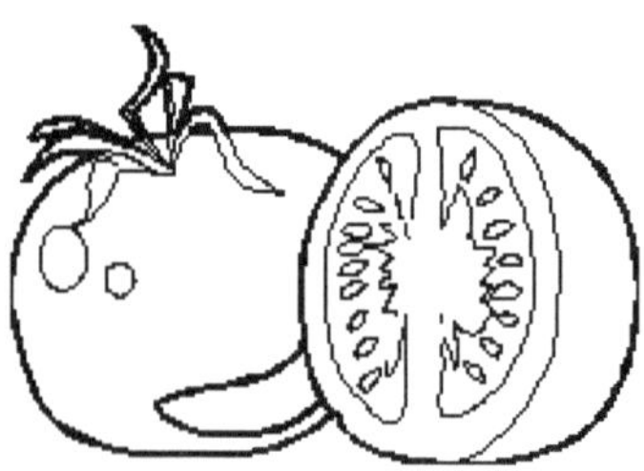

THE CAMP

I worked for one of the largest food companies in Canada. I was labeled as a troubleshooter or fixer-upper. It simply meant when a chef was taking his vacation, I had to take over his kitchen for one week to two months with little or no practice run to learn where the ingredients and the groceries were or the names of employees. It simply consisted of "Hi, François. I am the chef waiter Tom. Let me show you around."

The local chef usually gave me a quick tour and pointed out the fridge, freezer, dry-goods supply room, and kitchen staff changing room. It never failed that the chef's office was last, and he would add, "Here is the schedule, the menus for the week, and your list of local suppliers. See you in a month or so."

There I was. The cooking part was easy, but administration as well as remembering the employees' names, the whereabouts of equipment, supplies, etc., was difficult. They used me for all occasions — a birth in the chef's family, sick leave when he quit from pressure or personal problems, or a simple vacation. Organizing the food, labor, and figuring operating costs were my tasks. Maybe it was because I made it look easy that the company had me doing this for seven years. On the bright side, I got to visit every town in Canada, as well as every summer camp that the company managed — government, private, and charity camps.

One evening I received a phone call. "Hey François! We have a small problem. Horst got stuck in Germany."

"Good for him. Where does it leave me?"

"You are going to camp."

"When?"

"At the break of dawn."

"Okay. Which one?"

"The one on Lake Kashawashawisgamog."

"Great! What is my job?"

"Easy. Check the supplies when they arrive and store

everything. You have a crew already trained from last year."

At the first sign of daylight I was packed with my knives, chef uniforms, chef's bible *Te Repertoire de Cuisine,* and toothbrush. I put on my helmet and goggles, slipped on my gloves and started hauling on my 750cc BMW motorcycle. Let me tell you, it was not easy to admire the sunrise, morning dew and awakening of nature at 100 mph on narrow side roads, but what a powerful feeling of freedom I had. My first task after arriving at camp was to wash the bugs off my face; next, I had a coffee and got acquainted with the rest of the crew.

Nadine was in charge. She had done a good job. The dining room was ready to go for the next day. Staples were stocked up, and perishables were in the fridge. "At what time will the children arrive tomorrow?" I asked candidly.

"They will be here at 6 p.m. tonight."

"No one said anything about tonight. The boss said tomorrow at noon."

"Wrong info. Their leader phoned last night for confirmation."

"Swell. We make them hamburgers tonight, and French toast for the morning."

"Good enough. Sounds easy to me. I'll get Susan to make the salad."

"How many kids, Nadine?"

"Four hundred fifty, including the chaperons." Calculating 1½ hamburgers per kid and 2 per adult, it was 750 hamburgers — an easy job, providing the equipment was working. I took time to get settled into my room, which did not take long since it was only for two days. I was back in the kitchen where our aspiring dishwasher had prepared omelets for lunch, trying to get promoted to breakfast cook. I learned later in the season that he got his promotion.

At 2 p.m. we got a phone call. "Chef, it is for you," shouted Susan from the back office.

"Somebody already knew about my arrival," I thought while getting the receiver. "Chef here."

"Horst?"

"No, he is stuck on the other side of the puddle."

"François, my favorite crook! Sam here. How have you been?"

"Scattered all over Ontario, as usual."

"Still driving your black beast?"

"Yes. I even had it souped up. Why? You want to buy it?"

"No. Listen. My truck is broken down over 150 miles from you. I cannot deliver the meat until tomorrow noon."

"Super! What do I feed my kids?"

"Got to go. See you tomorrow."

"That's right, Sam. Run away. See you at noon." It's amazing how a phone call can pass on problems to another person. "Nadine!" I screamed. "Get over here!"

"What?"

"We've got troubles."

She was over in the office in three leaps. "Shoot."

"We aren't going to get the meat. The truck has broken down."

She looked at me and paused a few seconds. "I am so glad I am not the chef." Somehow I felt it was not going to be the easiest day in my life. "Let's make them the French toast tonight and scrambled eggs for the morning," she said.

"They have been on busses all day. We need to give them real food. I am going to check the freezer." Nadine followed me only to see the look of surprise on my face when I realized how empty it was in there. I kicked around the couple of cardboard boxes, mainly leftover scraps from last year, frozen in time and waiting for a good soul to get rid of them. I pulled out a large box. "A cooked turkey?"

"Yes. There is one more right over here."

I looked in the rest of the containers, nothing that would feed 450 screaming kids. There wasn't even enough either to grind up meat for Bolognese sauce — just two small turkeys. It was time to do some creative thinking.

Nadine came back into the freezer pushing a cart, yanking me out of my thoughts. I loaded the two boxes on the cart and cut them in half on the meat saw. I put the turkeys in the oven at 150 degrees to thaw them out. Then I cooked them with celery, onions, sprouts and whatever I could find. Needless to say, that evening the chaperons and children ate the best chow mein ever. Very little meat was to be found, but a full belly does not ask questions. Also, panicking has never helped in a kitchen, except for getting cut or burned, so stay calm and get creative!

Quiches

QUICHES

Quiches are a great way to use leftovers without being obvious. Serve them for a late breakfast or brunch on the weekend, a light lunch, an early evening meal, or midnight snack. Throw a fruit medley together to look pretty on the plate and "real men do eat quiche". With the following simple recipes, they can cook the quiche themselves.

QUICHE LORRAINE

- 1 pie shell from your grocer's freezer (Believe me, it is good and obviously faster than making your own. Deep-dish works better, if they have it.)
- 8 ounces shredded cheese (your favorite cheddar, Monterrey Jack, or mozzarella)
- 1 onion, sliced
- ½ pound bacon, diced
- 4 eggs
- 1 pint milk (or ½ pint milk and ½ pint whipping cream.)
- A dash nutmeg to taste

Sauté the bacon and onions in a frying pan (do not use oil or butter — the bacon has enough oil by itself). Drain the fat and let it cool off. Mix the bacon, onions and cheese together in a bowl. This is a personal trick I apply to all my quiches. It prevents having all the ingredients on the bottom while the cheese floats to the top. Mix the milk, eggs, and nutmeg. Notice that there is no salt. The cheese and bacon have enough to flavor the rest. Put the cheese, bacon, and onions in the pie shell. Gently pour in the egg and milk mixture. Put it in the oven on a cookie sheet to prevent spillage. Bake at 350 degrees until golden brown and the egg mixture firms up. It should take approximately 30 to 35 minutes.

QUICHE PROVINCIAL

- ☐ 1 tablespoon oil
- ☐ 1 small onion, chopped
- ☐ 4 to 5 sliced mushrooms
- ☐ ½ teaspoon thyme
- ☐ 2 garlic cloves, chopped
- ☐ 2 small tomatoes, diced
- ☐ 3 green onions (called spring onions or scallions also), sliced or chopped
- ☐ 8 ounces shredded cheese
- ☐ 1 pint milk
- ☐ 1 small green pepper, chopped
- ☐ 4 eggs
- ☐ 1 large pie shell, unsweetened

Mix the eggs and milk together. Sauté the onions, green pepper, mushrooms and thyme in oil for 4 to 5 minutes. Add the garlic. Cool it off. Put it into a bowl with the tomato and cheese and blend. Pack it into the pie shell. Pour in the milk and eggs gently. Put it into a preheated oven at 350 degrees and bake until it is golden brown and the egg mixture firms up. It should take approximately 30 to 35 minutes.

MUSHROOM QUICHE

- ☐ 1 pie shell
- ☐ 8 ounces mushrooms, sliced
- ☐ 1 small onion, chopped
- ☐ 1 tablespoon oil
- ☐ 4 eggs
- ☐ 1 pint milk
- ☐ 8 ounces shredded cheese
- ☐ A dash nutmeg to taste

Sauté the onion and mushrooms in a frying pan with the oil. Proceeding the same as for Quiche Lorraine or Quiche Provincial, putting cooled onions and mushrooms with cheese into the pie shell and pour the mixture of eggs, nutmeg, and milk on top. Bake at 350 until golden brown (about 30 to 35 minutes).

SHRIMP QUICHE

- ☐ 1 pie shell
- ☐ 8 to 10 ounces salad shrimp
- ☐ 1 small onion, chopped
- ☐ 1 tablespoon parsley
- ☐ 2 garlic cloves, chopped
- ☐ 1 tablespoon oil
- ☐ 4 eggs
- ☐ 1 pint milk
- ☐ 8 ounces shredded cheese
- ☐ A dash nutmeg to taste

Sauté the onion in the oil for 4 to 5 minutes. Add the chopped garlic and shrimp and cook for a minute only. Add the parsley and sprinkle with a touch of salt. Remember not to add too much salt because the cheese is salty enough. Also, a dash Worcestershire sauce is good in it. Cool it off and mix in the cheese. Proceed the same as for Quiche Lorraine. Pour it into the pie crust. Mix the eggs, milk, and nutmeg and pour it over the cooked solids. Bake until golden brown (about 30 to 35 minutes) at 350 degrees.

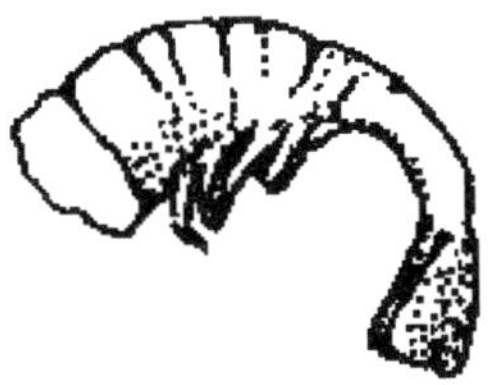

BROCCOLI QUICHE

- 4 eggs
- 1 pint milk
- 8 ounces shredded cheese
- 6 to 8 ounces broccoli buds
- A dash nutmeg to taste

Bring water to a boil. Add the broccoli to the boiling water and cook 2 to 3 minutes. Drain the water. Proceed the same as for Quiche Lorraine. Put the broccoli and cheese in the pie shell and pour the liquid mixture on top. Bake until golden brown (about 30 to 35 minutes) in a preheated oven at 350 degrees.

Quiches with asparagus, fiddle head, mixed vegetables, or a medley are all made the same way.

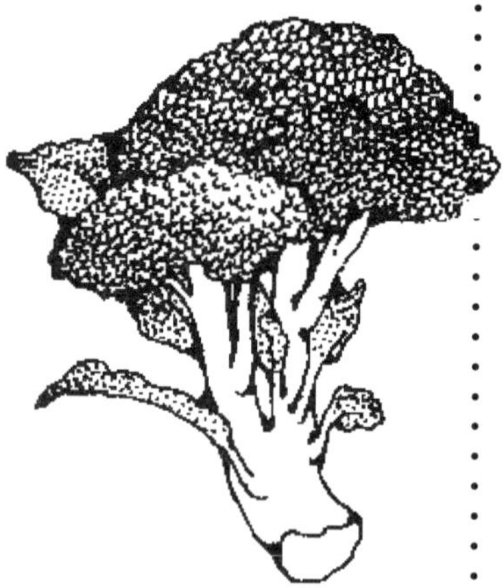

CLAM QUICHE

- ☐ 1 small onion, chopped
- ☐ 2 four-ounce cans baby clams (drain the juice and keep it in the freezer for when you make the Chowders beginning on page 54)
- ☐ ¼ teaspoon thyme
- ☐ 1 tablespoon oil
- ☐ 4 eggs
- ☐ 1 pint milk
- ☐ 8 ounces shredded cheese
- ☐ 6 to 8 ounces broccoli buds
- ☐ A dash nutmeg to taste

Sauté the onion in the oil for about 5 minutes. Add the garlic and the clams (do not cook, just mix). Put in a bowl and add the cheese. Proceed the same as Quiche Lorraine. Also, smoked salmon, smoked trout, smoked turkey, or smoked oysters can all be used in the same fashion. Do not cook it in the frying pan. Just mix it with the cheese.

For quiche made with fish, salmon, or bay scallops, the meat must be cooked for 1 to 2 minutes in the pan mixed with onion, a touch of chopped parsley or sliced green onions. No garlic, please. The fish must be in slivers or diced. Bay scallops are small enough.

Also you can try quiche with ham, breakfast sausage, leftover chopped Thanksgiving turkey, chopped chicken, or even a combination of the above. The secret is 1 pint of milk for 4 eggs. Or, ½ pint milk and ½ pint 35% cream is a stunningly smooth, light, delectable combination. Go ahead. Indulge!

Rice Dishes

RICE DISHES

Rice has been a staple in the food history of the world since 3000 B.C. In Chinese the word "rice" actually means "agriculture" or "culture". There are basically three kinds of rice which are long, medium, and short grain. The long grain is the most fluffy when cooked. I prefer the parboiled or converted rice, not only because it is usually fortified with additional vitamins, but it also seems to adapt itself to a variety of dishes.

PERFECT RICE

You will never miss. Also, it will be easy for reheating or preparing leftovers.

- ☐ 1 cup rice
- ☐ 2 cups water
- ☐ 2 chicken bouillon cubes

Mix rice and water together in a pan and stir. Bring it to a boil and add 2 chicken bouillon cubes and stir well. Lower the heat and cover with a lid. Simmer covered for approximately 15 to 18 minutes. It is that simple. I prefer parboiled rice, not so much for the taste but because it is so versatile, and it has no limits.

PERFECT RICE VARIATION

- ☐ 1 cup rice
- ☐ 1 cup water
- ☐ 1 cup white wine
- ☐ 2 chicken bouillon cubes

The cooking instructions are the same as for Perfect Rice.

MUSHROOM RICE

- ☐ 1 cup rice
- ☐ 2 cups water or 1 cup water and 1 cup white wine
- ☐ 1 small onion, chopped
- ☐ 1 pint (8 ounces) pre-sliced mushrooms from your grocery store
- ☐ 1 tablcspoon butter
- ☐ 2 chicken bouillon cubes

Melt the butter; add the onions and cook 2 to 3 minutes. Do not let it get brown. Add the mushrooms and cook 2 more minutes; while stirring add the water and rice and 2 chicken bouillon cubes. Bring to a boil, lower the heat, cover, and simmer 15 to 18 minutes.
Rice made with bacon, ham or smoked turkey is handled the same as Mushroom Rice or Leek Rice.

ASPARAGUS RICE

- ☐ 1 bunch (about 1 pound) asparagus
- ☐ 1 cup rice
- ☐ 2 cups water
- ☐ 2 bouillon cubes (chicken or beef)

Bring the water, rice, and bouillon cubes to a boil. Cut fresh asparagus into 1-inch lengths, discarding the lower third of the root. Add the asparagus when it starts boiling, lower the heat, cover, and simmer 15 to 18 minutes.

For canned asparagus you must drain the juice from the asparagus. Replace part of the water with the asparagus juice, if possible. Cut the asparagus into 1-inch pieces and mix gently into the cooked rice.

ALMOND RICE

- ☐ 1 cup rice
- ☐ 2 cups water
- ☐ 2 bouillon cubes
- ☐ ½ cup sliced almonds

Bring rice, water, cubes to a boil. Add ½ cup of sliced almonds. Lower heat, cover, and simmer for 15 to 18 minutes. This is good with fish or chicken with a sweet gravy base, and also for curry dishes.
Walnut Rice is the same procedure as Almond Rice.

BROCCOLI RICE

- ☐ 1 cup rice
- ☐ 2 cups water
- ☐ 2 beef or chicken bouillon cubes
- ☐ 1 cup broccoli buds

Bring all but the broccoli to a boil. Lower the heat, cover and simmer for 12 to 15 minutes. Add the broccoli and simmer covered for another 5 minutes.

LEEK RICE

- ☐ 1 to 1½ pounds leeks
- ☐ 1 cup rice
- ☐ 2 cups water
- ☐ 2 bouillon cubes (beef or chicken)

Thoroughly wash, cut, and finely chop leeks. Sauté them in a pan with 1 tablespoon of butter or oil (no olive oil — it overpowers the rice dish) for 3 to 4 minutes. Add 2 cups water (or 1 cup water and 1 cup wine), 1 cup rice, and 2 bouillon cubes. Bring it to a boil and mix. Lower the heat, cover, and simmer for 15 to 18 minutes.

More suggestions to trigger your imagination :

Replace the leeks with finely chopped green romaine, zucchini, spinach, or celery. Also, red or green peppers can be added during the last 5 minutes of cooking plain rice to add zing. Add a can of diced artichokes, peas, whole corn kernels, or chopped red pepper to give it life. Change the texture by adding a teaspoon of curry or tarragon in the last 5 minutes. Again, use your imagination and leftovers.

TOMATO RICE

- ☐ 1 cup rice
- ☐ 2 cups water
- ☐ 2 bouillon cubes
- ☐ 2 medium tomatoes, diced

Bring water, rice and bouillon cubes to a boil. Reduce the heat and simmer covered for 10 to 12 minutes. Add the diced tomatoes and simmer 5 minutes more.

LEFTOVER RICE

Now let us move on to leftover rice. It works with all the above from mushroom to broccoli. I would perhaps exclude the Almond Rice or Walnut Rice, but use your imagination.

Bacon, ham, or smoked turkey rice are all the same technique. Sauté bacon to the crispness of your choice. Add the rice and sauté while stirring from time to time until warm. Put it on a plate *et voila*! If it is Broccoli Rice or Asparagus Rice, add one or two diced tomatoes. Even a can of drained peas will do. Or cook a couple of fried eggs in a separate pan, and put the eggs on top of your pile of rice with a couple pieces of toast. You'll be set for several hours.

Another way to enhance leftover rice is to add a can of tuna to your rice. You can also chop up leftover chicken breast or turkey from Thanksgiving. Add tomato sauce for variety.

How about adding chopped up breakfast sausage links or patties, or try two sliced hot dogs to stretch the leftovers? You see, all combinations are welcome.

THE EMPEROR

Many years ago I had the pleasure to cook for a highly regarded dignitary, Emperor Haile Selassie, the ruler of Ethiopia for fifty-three years. At the time I was too young to pay any attention to world politics so I wasn't overly impressed. At my young age of nineteen, even the next morning had no relevancy. Many years later in Toronto, Canada, where I had decided to set up my tent, I was discussing the menu for the upcoming banquet in honor of Bill Davis, the Prime Minister of Ontario. The conversation turned to the importance of our task when I said a couple of sentences about having cooked for other dignitaries, so that the staff would feel confident that we could do a good job. Someone asked me to name some of these renowned personalities. Needless to say, my vanity kicked into high gear giving me the urge to recite all the known persons from actors, singers, and sports people that I could remember. Sensing that the whole restaurant staff was hanging on to my every word, my ego was totally out of control.

It came as a surprise when the mentioning of Emperor Haile Selassie caused a gentleman named Mustapha to jump out of his chair. He leaped toward me and landed on his knees, bowing and kissing both my hands, repeating, "You have served His Majesty!" For the next two weeks, a dozen or so people of Ethiopian descent came by the restaurant to introduce themselves and to pay their respect to me as one of the last persons who had contact with their beloved Emperor. It was a great honor and a humbling experience, although the embarrassment made it a little uncomfortable for me at the time.

Pastas

PASTA

Pasta is available in many shapes and forms. My favorites are penne and bow tie, because they are easy to handle and mix easily with sauces. They are also easy to toss (which is right up my alley) in the frying pan without making a mess.

Cook your favorite brand penne according to the label. When cooked, chilled off and drained, put a wet cloth on top of it to prevent it from drying out while you are preparing the sauce. Here are various ways to quickly enhance the penne pasta.

PENNE WITH BACON

- ½ pound bacon cut into small pieces

Sauté the bacon in a frying pan to your taste (some like the bacon soft; others like it crisp or extra crunchy). Do not put oil in the frying pan because the bacon has plenty of fat. Add about 3 or 4 cups of the cooked penne and toss well. Serve hot with a sprinkle of Parmesan or chopped parsley for color. You can substitute your bacon with ham, turkey (plain or smoked), or breakfast sausage patties or links cut in small pieces.

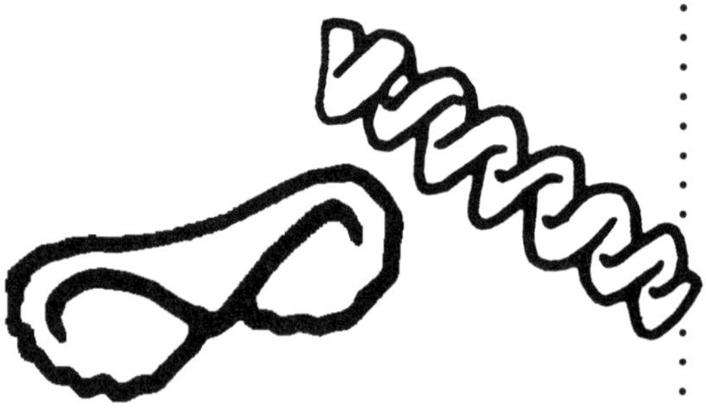

PENNE WITH TUNA (Serves 4)

- ☐ 1 small onion, chopped
- ☐ 3 to 4 medium tomatoes, diced, or one can tomato sauce
- ☐ 1 to 2 cans of tuna (3 for me since I like tuna)
- ☐ 1 tablespoon olive oil
- ☐ 4 garlic cloves, thinly sliced or chopped
- ☐ Salt to taste

Cook the penne according to the label. Sauté the onion with the oil for 2 to 3 minutes. Add the tomato, garlic, and drained tuna (flake or solid). Simmer covered for 5 minutes at low heat. Add 3 or 4 cups of the cooked penne and toss well. Add salt to taste and simmer until the pasta is warm.

NOTE : You can replace the tuna with ham, bacon, turkey, Polish sausage, or chicken leftovers. Remember, creating is the way to go. Throw in tarragon, black olives, or leftover cooked broccoli. Be bold! Be daring! Create a new gourmet dish!

PENNE CARBONARA (my version)

- ☐ 6 to 8 ounces sliced ham (any brand), coarsely chopped
- ☐ 1 tablespoon butter or oil
- ☐ ½ pint heavy cream (35%)
- ☐ Parmesan cheese to taste

First, melt the butter in a large skillet. Add the ham and sauté for 1 to 2 minutes. Add the cream and bring it to a boil. Add the precooked penne pasta and cook at low heat until warm and well blended. Add salt, if necessary. Remember, some ham and the cheese might be salty enough. Serve hot after sprinkling on the grated Parmesan.

PENNE CARBONARA (Second version)

- 6 to 8 ounces coarsely chopped ham
- 2 eggs, well beaten
- 1 tablespoon Parmesan
- 1 pinch salt
- 1 tablespoon butter

Precook the penne pasta; drain it and set it aside. Melt the butter in a skillet or frying pan. Add the ham to it and sauté until it starts softening up and begins to sizzle. Add the penne, blend and cook covered at low heat. Whisk the 2 eggs together with the Parmesan cheese. When the penne and ham are hot, remove the lid and mix one more time. Pour in the egg and Parmesan cheese mixture and cook 2 to 3 minutes until the egg starts to scramble, stirring constantly. Ring the bell for dinner while it is hot.

LEFTOVER SPAGHETTI NOODLES

Whip 2 to 3 whole eggs and blend with 2 cups randomly chopped spaghetti. Add salt and pepper. Put the mixture in a preheated frying pan (Teflon is better) and cook for 3 to 4 minutes. Flip over (if necessary get help from a spatula) and cook further until it is golden brown. Serve hot, topped with tomato sauce.

You can also try enhancing with chopped precooked breakfast sausage, or precooked green pepper, bacon, chopped broccoli, or asparagus. It is good for Sunday brunch.

Vegetables

CARROTS (Serves 4)

I do not like carrots but they are good for us, so I eat them at least once a week. Here is how I prepare them. Calculate approximately 3 ounce of carrots per person.

- ☐ 12 ounces carrots
- ☐ 1 tablespoon butter
- ☐ 1 pan with a tight lid
- ☐ 1 small onion, sliced
- ☐ 1 cup white wine
- ☐ Salt to taste

Slice the carrots. Put the butter, onion, and carrots in the pan and add the cup of wine. Simmer covered for 20 minutes at low heat. Add salt to taste. After the carrots are cooked you can add white pepper, but not during cooking.
* Never put pepper on carrots while they are cooking — it makes them bitter.

HONEY CARROTS (Serves 4)

- ☐ 12 ounces sliced carrots
- ☐ 1 tablespoon butter
- ☐ 3 large teaspoons honey
- ☐ ¼ cup water

Put the butter, carrots, honey and ¼ cup water in a pan with a tightfitting lid. Cook covered for 20 minutes at low heat. You are done. Try replacing the honey with white grape jelly, fig jam, apricot preserves, or even gooseberry preserves.

Never put pepper on carrots while they are cooking — it makes them bitter.

CREAMED CARROTS (Serves 4)

- ☐ 12 ounces diced or sliced carrots (also, finger or baby carrots will do)
- ☐ ½ pint whipping cream
- ☐ 1 heaping tablespoon flour
- ☐ ¼ teaspoon nutmeg
- ☐ 1 cup water
- ☐ A dash Worcestershire sauce to taste

Cook the carrots in about ½ cup water for about 20 minutes in a covered pan on low heat. Remove carrots and keep the liquid. Mix remainder of original cool water into the flour slowly until smooth, and then whisk it into the boiling carrot liquid. Add nutmeg, Worcestershire sauce, and 1 to 2 tablespoons cream. Use the rest of the cream for your favorite coffee. Mix the carrots into the cream sauce and toss gently.

- ☑ Never put pepper on carrots while they are cooking — it makes them bitter.

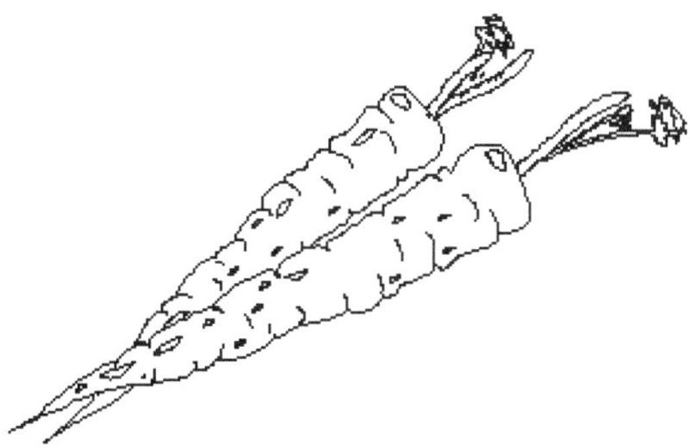

SAUTEED SPINACH

- ☐ 2 bunches spinach
- ☐ 1 beef bouillon cube
- ☐ ½ teaspoon minced or chopped garlic (the prepared garlic in a jar, all chopped and minced is fine)
- ☐ ½ cup water

Wash and dry the spinach. In a frying pan or a low broiler pan mix the water, the beef bouillon cube, and the garlic. Bring it to a boil. Add the spinach and cook covered 10 minutes at low heat. Mix the spinach once during the process. Serve hot.

LEFTOVERS : Warm it up in the zapper (microwave) and top with 2 fried eggs. *Et viola* — Eggs Florentine!

You can do the same with frozen spinach. Just remember to take it out of the freezer the night before. When thawed, squeeze out the excess water with your hands and then proceed the same as with fresh spinach.

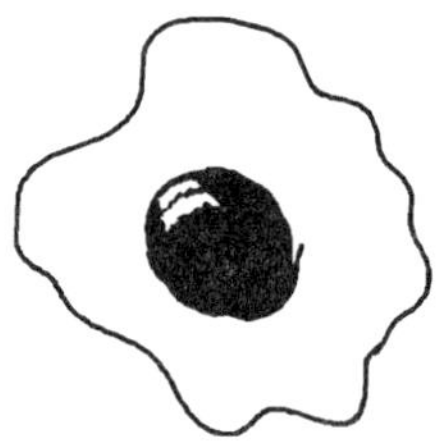

BLACK-EYED PEAS

The first time I visited the South was around the Christmas holidays. One of the traditions that I was not familiar with was the foods that were eaten on New Year's Day. "I'll have to stay home all day. It is my turn to cook the black-eyed peas," my friend lamented.

"Why all day?" I asked.

"It takes hours to soak them and forever to cook them," she replied.

"Do you mind if I give it a shot?"

"By all means!"

"Good, leave the black-eyes to me," I answered realizing that I had never cooked a black-eyed pea in my life. My advantage was that I was trained as a chef. So after a quick trip to the store, I came up with the dish on the next page that had everyone asking for the recipe.

BLACK-EYED PEAS (Serves 4)

- ☐ 1 tablespoon olive or other oil
- ☐ 1 onion, chopped
- ☐ 1 pound bacon (whole, not sliced, if possible)
- ☐ ½ teaspoon oregano
- ☐ ½ teaspoon thyme
- ☐ 1 can tomato sauce, 8 ounces
- ☐ 2 cans black-eyed peas, 15 ounces each
- ☐ 4 cloves garlic (sliced or chopped)

Cut the bacon into ½-inch to 1-inch squares. Wash and drain the black-eyed peas. Sauté the oil, bacon, onion, oregano, and thyme 4 to 5 minutes until the onions are cooked but not brown. Add the garlic and tomato sauce. (Garlic is never cooked with the onion. It cannot tolerate the high temperature and will turn black and have an unpleasantly bitter taste.) Add the black-eyed peas. Stir well and simmer 15 minutes at low temperature. *Et voila*! In 20 minutes you have yourself a perfect New Year tradition. For seasoning I use a bit of salt and liquid amino acid which adds a fantastic taste to food without MSG and other additives.

Amino acid has no MSG or other additives. It's great for flavoring just about everything!

MASHED POTATOES

- ☐ 3 pounds potatoes, cleaned, peeled, and cut in halves or quarters
- ☐ 1 cup milk (whole or 2%)
- ☐ 2 tablespoons butter
- ☐ 1 pinch nutmeg
- ☐ ½ teaspoon salt

Put the potatoes in a pan and add water until they are covered. Add the salt and bring it to a boil. Reduce to simmer, cover with a lid, and simmer gently 15 to 18 minutes. Turn off the heat and let it sit 10 minutes.

Drain the potatoes in a colander. In the meantime, put the milk in a small pan with the butter. Put the pan on the stove and warm it almost to a boil. Put the potatoes back into the original cooking pan and sprinkle the nutmeg over it. Add the warm milk and mash gently until the milk, butter and potatoes are well blended. Using a whisk, most of the chunks will be gone. If it is too thick, add milk, only one tablespoon at a time since it is easy to add, and impossible to remove.

BRUSSELS SPROUTS

I don't like Brussels sprouts. As a matter of fact, I hate Brussels sprouts. This is the only way I will eat them. Try it. You will like it.

- 8 ounces Brussels sprouts (fresh or frozen)
- ½ small onion, finely chopped
- ¼ pound sliced bacon
- Salt and pepper to taste
- Nutmeg to taste

Slice the bacon into tiny ½-inch strips. Put the bacon in a frying pan. Add the onion and cook until onion is soft, and bacon is starting to get crisp (do not overcook, please!). Put the Brussels sprouts in boiling water and cook them for 5 minutes. Drain the Brussels sprouts. Mix them with the onion and bacon and toss it well. Sprinkle with salt to your taste. Don't forget, bacon has salt also. Sprinkle with nutmeg just before serving.

The same recipe can apply for cooking the wonderful Canadian fiddle head.

AU GRATIN POTATOES

- ☐ ½ pounds potatoes
- ☐ ¼ ounce ground nutmeg
- ☐ 1 pint whipping cream (35%)
- ☐ 8 ounces grated cheese
- ☐ Salt and white pepper to taste

Peel, wash, and dry the potatoes. Slice them in a food processor or by hand as thin as possible (don't cut yourself now). Remember to use a sharp knife. Don't wash them after slicing because you need the starch to act as a binder. Put the sliced potatoes in a bowl and add salt, nutmeg, and white pepper (black pepper leaves unpleasant spots) and toss. Put a dab of oil or butter in an oven roasting pan and grease it well with your fingers, a paper towel, or a pastry brush (I use my finger; it is, after all, our best tool). Put all the potatoes in the roasting pan. Add the whipping cream and bake in a preheated oven at 375 degrees for 45 minutes. Pull it out of the oven after 30 minutes and sprinkle cheese all over it. Push it back into the oven, lower the heat to 325 degrees and bake for another 15 minutes.

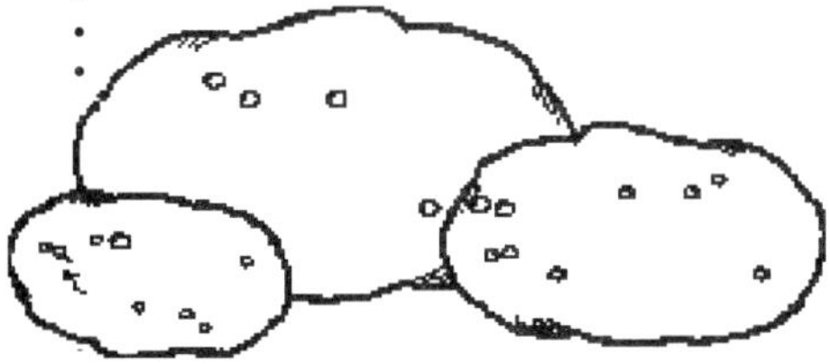

Entrees

PORK CUTLETS WITH *CHARCUTIERE* GRAVY

- 4 pork cutlets (chops) or pork loin steaks
- 2 heaping tablespoons flour
- 2 large eggs
- 1 package bread crumbs from your store (any flavor)
- 1 pinch salt
- 4 tablespoons oil

Whisk the egg in a large bowl with a pinch of salt. Spread the flour on a platter and flour the pork cutlets on each side lightly. Shake off the excess and discard the flour. Put the cutlets in the bowl with the eggs and turn them very gently until they are moist all over. The flour will make the egg wash stick.

Now put the bread crumbs in a cake pan which has a high rim. Take one cutlet and hold it up a few seconds to drain the excess egg; then put it in the bread crumbs and cover it well with the crumbs. Pound the cutlet gently but firmly. Flip the cutlet over and do it again. It will seal the cutlet well. Pick it up gently, shake the excess crumbs off, and put it on a plate. Prepare all the cutlets like this for cooking.

Heat oil in the frying pan on the stove. Put a wooden spoon in the oil; when the wood starts making bubbles, it is hot enough to start cooking. Cook the cutlets on each side until golden brown. Depending on the size of your frying pan, cook 2, 3, or 4 at the same time. Put the cutlets in the 250-degree preheated oven for 10 minutes. Discard the oil.

CHARCUTIERE SAUCE

- □ 1 pack brown gravy
- □ 1 to 2 teaspoons quality mustard
- □ 1 medium crisp Kosher or dill pickle in thin strips or thin slices

Cook the gravy according to the directions. Whisk the mustard into the gravy. Add the pickles and cook one more minute. If you like, you can replace half of the water that goes into the gravy mix with white wine. A tablespoon or so of whipping cream can be mixed into the gravy to make it more velvety.

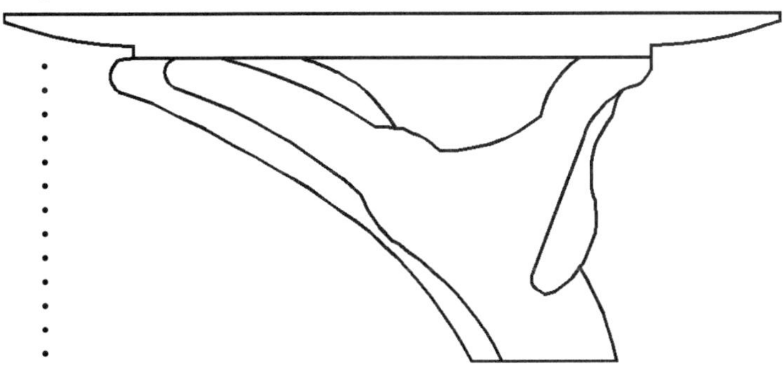

STUFFED ZUCCHINI (Serves 4)

- ☐ 4 large green or yellow zucchinis
- ☐ 8 ounces ground meat (beef, pork, or turkey; I like ostrich)
- ☐ ¼ teaspoon thyme
- ☐ 6 to 8 mushrooms
- ☐ 1 small onion
- ☐ 1 to 2 ounces cheese
- ☐ ½ tablespoon oil
- ☐ 2 small tomatoes, chopped
- ☐ 4 garlic cloves, peeled and chopped
- ☐ Salt to taste

Put water on the stove in a large pan. Cut the zucchinis lengthwise and hollow them out. Keep the inside of the zucchinis. Chop the onion fairly small (I won't come to check, so don't worry). Chop the mushrooms. When the water boils, add the zucchinis and cook them for 2 minutes. Take them out and put them on a paper towel upside down to drain. Put a skillet or frying pan on the burner with the oil. Add the onion, thyme and ground meat, and cook for approximately 5 minutes. Separate the meat with a wooden spoon while cooking. Add the chopped mushrooms, garlic, and tomatoes. Chop the inside parts of the zucchini you took out from the center and add it to the ingredients cooking in the skillet.

Put the zucchinis on a baking sheet with the hollow side up and fill them with the ingredients from the skillet. Sprinkle with cheese and cook for 5 to 8 minutes in a preheated oven of 350 degrees. A glass of red wine will taste good with it.

VARIATIONS : Add more mushrooms and use the stuffing for stuffed green pepper. Add olives if you wish, or even chopped celery. Replace the ground beef with tuna.

THE BEEFCAKES

Many years ago I was asked to replace a colleague way up in northern Ontario in a summer camp. It was a four-week assignment while he went to Europe for his summer vacation.

It seemed like an easy enough task; besides, it was a company I had worked for several times in other types of operations. The only piece of advice I got from Tom was, "The beefcakes are coming, so make up a lot of food." First, I was in Canada less than one year; second, I had never heard the term "beefcake." Also, he gave me this information while he was passing through the border gate at the airport to which I had so kindly driven him.

From there I drove the 300 miles to the camp. It was right on a lake surrounded by giant maples, pines, and majestic birch trees in a wonderful secluded wilderness. After a 300-mile ride by myself, I had forgotten the words of my friend's warning. My only memory was "beef." So I mentioned it to my new assistant chef, a competent young man by the name of Arthur. "Arthur, what is the beef?"

He gave me a big smile and said, "Follow me." We ended up in the fridge where he showed me boxes of different cuts of beef. From there to the end of the freezer was a virtual mountain of boxes of all kinds of beef, chicken, fish, pork, and frozen vegetables.

"Good. We are set for the summer." I went to bed with a relieved conscience; besides, I was tired after my long ride.

The next morning I got up sort of late. Seven thirty a.m. was usually a treat for me. Coffee was brewing with Arthur running all over the kitchen arranging everything. The camp had been closed for one year, so all the equipment had to be washed. "Have a cup of coffee. I will join you in a few minutes," he said pointing to the coffee machine. As the new kid on the block, I decided to surrender to his advice and grabbed myself a cup of coffee and sat down. He came back shortly, holding his own steaming cup and asking, "Did you have a good night's rest?"

"Excellent, thank you. But tell me why everybody is running around."

"We have a small group tonight. I am organizing the kitchen so we can get ready for them."

"What can I do?" I asked.

"For starters, get unpacked and make yourself comfortable. Be back at noon for lunch. At 1:30 we start work."

"You don't need my help?"

"No. After all, only 160 people are showing up."

"Good. I'll be back at noon." I was young, but I was already handling crowds of 1,000 or more. So I went back to my quarters without further thought.

At noon all the dishwashers, pot washers, dining room help, and salad people had arrived. We had lunch like a great big happy family. I sat beside Arthur, who was still shouting orders around. "Hey Chef, grab yourself a plate of grub!" We engulfed our food in minutes and started to get to know each other. He was an English gentleman who had never attended school to learn the trade, but he sure had a talent for it.

"So, what is on the menu?" I asked.

"Rib eyes, roast potatoes, green beans, and ice cream for dessert. I kept it easy for all of us on the first day."

"Good. It will give me time to get used to the layout. Where do I start?"

"Nowhere. I have tonight under control. Get ready for the lunch menu tomorrow. One more thing. The breakfast cook will be here at four p.m."

"Experienced?"

"Yes. Twenty-six summers in the camp."

"No sweat." I went to look around my new office, and rearranged a few paper clips. I was ready to look at the lunch menu. There was no science to it — straightforward home cooking. A note had been posted from my friend, who came a week earlier to do the ordering, start up all the equipment, and receive the gas delivery. It already looked like vacation time for me. "Arthur, when is dinner exactly?"

"Six p.m., Boss. Don't worry. We are ready."

I went and double checked, just to be sure. After all, I was given an assignment. We had one more hour until dinner time. I looked at the food. It was great. The beans were tasty; the gravy was hot with perfect texture. Henry, the meat man, was tossing the rib eyes in the oven to keep them warm when it dawned on me.

"Arthur, what is with all the food?"

"The beefcakes are here," he replied calmly.

"That is the word I was looking for yesterday."

"You will find out in a few minutes." At six o'clock it sounded like a heard of buffalo charged in. Each grabbed a plate and took two to three rib eyes and piled beans and spuds on a different plate. It all went so fast! They were eating long before the dust had time to settle. Henry and Arthur stood beside me as I looked in horror at how they were stuffing their faces. *Moi*, a gourmet chef used to finicky people eating with the tip of their silverware! Here I was looking at a hoard of massive Vikings stuffing their faces like farmers shoving hay to their livestock with pitchforks. My eyes were bugging out of my head as Arthur slapped my shoulder. "Meet the Canadian Olympic wrestlers, weight lifters, Greco-Roman wrestlers, and their trainers." Talk about appetites! We had barely enough food for our own staff.

Arthur saved us. I would have cooked a conservative amount, creating a major friction for the rest of the evening. At ten p.m. we closed the dining room with the exception of a table of six who did not want to leave. Simon came to ask me what to do. "I asked them already four times. They refused," he said.

"I'll take care of it," I said. So, I went out to the dining room, looked at them, and asked politely in my broken English, "Gentlemen, we have an early rise tomorrow, so please leave."

The biggest one got up, a 350-pound weight lifter from Alberta. "Make me!" he said.

"Listen. You come outside. I will kick your butt so hard you won't be able to train for a week." What got into me, I never knew. He came right up to my face.

"Right now, Boy!" He turned around, walked out, and stood in the middle of the courtyard. "I'm waiting," he said as his buddy stood behind him.

"I'm coming," I replied, taking off my apron. Behind me the whole kitchen staff had become motionless, stunned by my skill to get in hot water at such speed. Personally, I had no idea of what was to happen next as I walked toward the door, firmly grabbing the handle while the sweat poured down my back and believe me, it was not from the heat. They were snickering and making remarks about my frail body frame. I opened the screen door and shouted at them, "Start fighting. I'll be there at eight a.m. after breakfast. Good night." I stepped back, slammed the door, and locked it as the giant jumped up on the front porch.

At seven a.m. the giant came straight to the kitchen to locate me, staring at my face. "My name is Moose. You handled yourself well. Thank you." We were friends for the rest of the time. Also, the rest of the kitchen staff breathed easier.

RIB EYE STEAKS SMOTHERED IN ONIONS (Serves 4)

- ☐ 4 well-marbled rib eye steaks (not too fatty)
- ☐ 3 large onions,sliced
- ☐ 1½ to 2 heaping tablespoons flour
- ☐ 1 pack brown gravy
- ☐ 1 cup red wine
- ☐ 1 cup white wine
- ☐ 2 garlic cloves, peeled and chopped
- ☐ 2 tablespoons oil (regular)

Peel the onions; cut them in half and slice them. Sauté them in a pan with 1 tablespoon oil until they are very soft and starting to turn brown. When they start to turn brown add 1 cup red wine, 1 cup white wine, and the garlic. Mix the gravy powder with water according to the instructions. Add the gravy to the onion and broth. When thickened, reduce the heat and simmer 10 to 12 minutes.

Put 1 tablespoon of oil in a frying pan. Preheat the pan until it starts to get red hot but not smoking. Sprinkle each steak with flour and dust off the excess. Cook them in the frying pan until golden brown. Flip the steaks over and repeat the process. When both sides are nice and brown, put the steaks on a plate and drain off the oil. Wipe the frying pan with a paper towel and put it back on the stove at low heat. Return the steaks to the pan without the oil. Pour the onion gravy all over them and cook for 4 to 5 minutes. Serve hot with mashed potatoes.

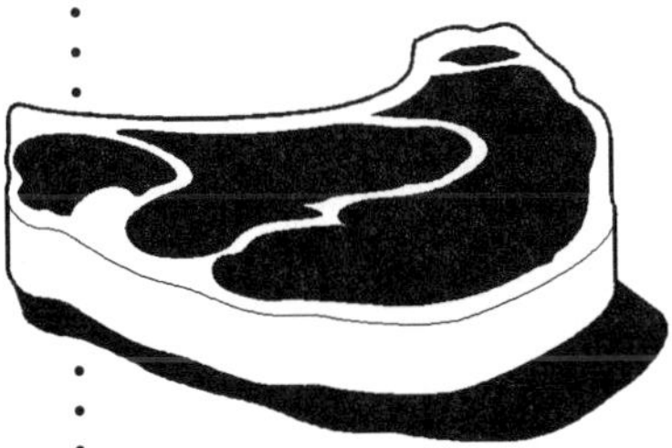

MEAT LASAGNA (Serves 4 to 6)

- ☐ 1 package lasagna noodles
- ☐ 2 pounds ground beef
- ☐ 2 teaspoons thyme
- ☐ 1 onion, chopped
- ☐ 1 pinch sugar
- ☐ 6 garlic cloves, or prepared minced garlic
- ☐ 6 tomatoes, diced
- ☐ 1 can (12 ounces) tomato sauce
- ☐ 16 ounces mushrooms, sliced
- ☐ 2 tablespoons oil
- ☐ 1 teaspoon oregano
- ☐ 1 tablespoon amino acid
- ☐ 4 green peppers, sliced (optional)
- ☐ Cheese to taste (grated mozzarella or your favorite)
- ☐ Salt and pepper to taste

Cook the lasagna noodles until done but firm, stirring often. Use a lot of water for two reasons: first, they won't break; second, they won't stick too much. When cooked, drain them over the sink and cool them off thoroughly. Add a tiny bit of oil and toss the noodles so they won't get glued together.

Mix the meat with one cup of water in a cooking pan. Bring it to a boil. When it starts boiling, mix one more time with a wooden spoon. Drain in a colander over the sink and rinse gently in cold water.

Put the pan back on the stove with the oil, chopped onion, and green pepper (optional) and cook for 4 to 5 minutes, stirring often. Add the mushrooms, thyme, and oregano and cook 2 more minutes. Add the chopped garlic, meat, and diced tomato; mix well. Add tomato sauce, salt, pepper, and amino acid and simmer 10 minutes. Now, let it cool.

After a cooling process (minimum 1 hour), proceed like all regular lasagna. Grease a four-inch-deep casserole or oven pan well and layer the lasagna, meat sauce, and cheese. I did not mark how much cheese; it is up to you — every layer, every second layer, or just on the top. For me, it gets to be everywhere.

THE DISCO

In my younger days I specialized in opening restaurants, clubs, discos, and trendy eateries. Back in 1978 when discos were ruling the music scene, I got a challenging job to start up a new project, a 12,000-square foot disco overlooking Toronto. We were on top of a hill on one of the main arteries going straight to the center of town, making it a pretty sight at night with all the moving lights from the traffic as well as buildings and houses. The restaurant had a seating area for 225 people, two bars, and a dance floor. It was lit up from above as well as from below since the floor was transparent plexiglass. It was state-of-the-art lighting and entertainment at its best, and I was proud to be a part of it.

My wife at the time was also a chef, and we worked together. She was my executive chef. We were in love and happy to be working together.

The excitement of construction, creating the menu, writing the recipes, hiring the staff, training the new crew, and getting close to the deadline was heaven. The opening day we served hot and cold *hors d'oeuvres* to a crowd of 300 reporters, media, Toronto swingers, and young executives. It was the second disco to open in Toronto, but it was number one for its strobe lighting, sheer size, and the innovative dance floor. The music was loud, but as clear as could be. Needless to say, the success was instantaneous.

The restaurant was three feet above the dance floor overlooking the action in a horseshoe shape. The music was horrendously loud, but the diners did not seem to mind. This was "the place" to be seen, so a little noise was not going to stop the guests who wanted to rub elbows with celebrities. We had lines of waiting customers every night.

I loved my work. The employees did a great job. My wife was beside me. Everywhere I went people knew I was the executive chef at The Disco. The food, pay, and working conditions were excellent. The menu prices were fairly steep which was expected at such a trendy place where the belief was, "If it is too cheap, it cannot be the best." So believe me, it was the best in every way.

The city danced to the tunes of Gloria Gaynor, Donna Summer, and many other artists. I even had the pleasure of cooking for Isaac Hayes, Barry White, and Yvonne de Carlos. Elton John dropped in one evening, which sent a wave of admiration out to the disco community.

It had taken us four months of preparation to build it, train the staff, get all the food and labor costs in place, and hire the electricians to get the dance area working. The results were stunning, a flaming overnight success. It was packed every day for lunch and dinner. The dance floor stayed full, and it took two massive men at the entrance to control the crowd.

Late one evening on a packed night I walked to the front door from the inside of the club. I was waiting for my wife while she gave her last instructions to the night shift, when two large individuals came up the stairwell that we kept clear for emergency evacuations. "Gentlemen, you have to wait at the end of the line," our first doorman said politely while the second doorman stood just behind him.

"We are here to see the owner."

"He is not here at the moment. As a matter of fact, I don't think he will show up tonight."

"We want to verify it for ourselves," the man continued.

"I don't think so," replied our doorman. The two strangers did not waste any more words. In a split second one gun was under the chin of the first doorman while the second thug promptly extended his arm, holding a black weapon and pressing it against the temple of the second security man. The doormen were as white as marshmallows. The one with his chin pushed up whispered, "Go in. The place is yours." I was frozen, hoping to blend into the darkness of the freshly decorated wall.

As the two gentlemen walked into the disco, my wife arrived saying, "Hi, Honey. I am ready. Let's go." I did not respond, my throat dry from the bold act of aggression. "Are you okay?" she asked, watching me as we walked out the door.

"Guess so, considering we are looking for a new job." She looked at me with surprise, so I explained the turn of events. You see, my passion has always been cooking, but my life was more important than any recipe that I could have produced. I have since divorced and stopped cooking for restaurants and institutions, and at least I am here to tell the tale and lived to cook another day.

BOILED SHRIMP

I have seen people cooking shrimp countless times, and it amazes me when I see a person do it right. It is a rare occurrence, and it is so simple.

Mix 4 cups water with 1 tablespoon vinegar, 1 carrot, 1 onion, and 1 celery stalk. Bring it to a boil. Let it boil for 10 minutes to let the taste of the carrots, celery, and onion blend together. Put 1 to 2 pounds of shrimp in the broth and cook for one minute. Move the shrimp and broth from the burner; let it set for 2 minutes. Pack as much ice as you can in the pan with the shrimp to cool them off. If you drain the broth prior to putting the ice over the shrimp, they will taste bland, but if you put ice cubes in the broth together with the shrimp, the taste is phenomenal. Try it, and you will be amazed at the difference.

SAUTEED SHRIMP

It does not matter whether you sauté the shrimp with onion, mushrooms, capers, tomatoes, garlic, or gumbo, you always put the shrimp in last. I repeat, THE SHRIMP ARE ALWAYS PUT IN LAST. It only takes a few minutes to cook a shrimp — like 2 to 3 minutes, not 10 to 15 or 20 minutes, like I have seen people do so often.

SEAFOOD LASAGNA (Serves 12 to 16)

This is one of my favorites for a number of reasons. First, I like it. Second, everyone likes it. You will get complements out of this one; if not, feed them bread and water for one week. Most important, you can do it two days prior to entertaining and slide it in the oven the day of the festivities. No problem. You are the success of the party.

- ☐ 2 packages lasagna
- ☐ 2 pounds fish (cod, mahi mahi, or orange roughy), in slivers
- ☐ 2 pounds salmon (ask the attendant fish specialist in your store; they will skin and bone it for you)
- ☐ 2 pounds shrimp (baby shrimp looks like more)
- ☐ 3 cans baby clams
- ☐ 1 packet (8 ounces) fake crab from your grocer's fridge, chopped
- ☐ 2½ pints heavy cream
- ☐ 1 large onion
- ☐ 1 pound sliced mushrooms
- ☐ 2 teaspoons thyme
- ☐ 5 heaping tablespoons flour
- ☐ 4 cloves garlic
- ☐ 1 pound grated cheese (or 2 pounds for me)
- ☐ 2 tablespoons oil
- ☐ 4 chicken bouillon cubes
- ☐ A dash Worcestershire sauce to taste
- ☐ Salt and pepper to taste

Cook the lasagna noodles in a lot of water for two reasons: first, they won't break; second, they won't stick too much. Cook until it is done but firm, stirring often. Drain and cool thoroughly. Add a tiny bit of oil and toss the lasagna noodles so they won't get glued together.

In a large pan put oil, onion, thyme, and mushrooms. Sauté together, mixing with a large spoon. Open the cans of clams and drain the juice into the pan, but don't add the clams. Add the bouillon cubes, garlic, and 3 cups water. Bring it to a boil. Reduce the heat and simmer for five minutes.

Now, pay attention. First, put in the slivers of fish (any fish you like; I prefer cod, mahi mahi, orange roughy). Add the salmon (dice it first, please). When it starts bubbling, add the fake crab and move it to the side.

Mix 1 cup cold water into the flour until it has the thickness of molasses. Put your pan back on high. Whisk the water and flour slowly into the fish mixture until it gets the consistency of blue cheese salad dressing.

Now, put in the shrimps, clams, and cream; stir gently. Add salt, pepper, and Worcestershire sauce to taste. When it starts cooking, you are finished.

You all know the assembly process. Grease an oven pan four inches high, either your own or a disposable, or get 3 half pans and freeze one or two for another occasion. Put lasagna, fish sauce, cheese, and repeat. I do it 5 or 6 times. Bake 1 hour and 15 minutes at 375 degrees with a light aluminum cover on top so it won't dry the cheese. Grease the aluminum so the cheese won't get stuck. Do not press the aluminum. After baking for 1 hour 15 minutes, pull off the foil and bake for 15 minutes more. *Bon appetit*!

TROUT ALMONDINE (Serves 4)

- 4 fresh trout fillets, 8 to 10 ounces each
- 4 ounces almonds, sliced (1 packet)
- 2 tablespoons butter
- 1 tablespoon oil
- 3 heaping tablespoons flour
- ¼ cup chopped parsley
- A dash lemon juice to taste
- Salt and pepper to taste

Rinse the trout and dry them with a paper towel. Salt and pepper them. Squeeze the lemon juice all over them. Roll the trout in the flour and tap off the excess. Put the trout in a preheated frying pan and cook 3 to 4 minutes or until golden brown. Flip them over and again cook 3 to 4 minutes, until golden brown. Put the frying pan in a preheated oven and bake for 10 minutes at 350 degrees.

Put butter in a frying pan and add the sliced almonds; sauté at low heat until some (not all) turn brown. Divide into four equal parts over each trout and serve hot, after sprinkling the parsley on top for looks.

This recipe is good also for whitefish, walleye, cod, hake, sole, mahi mahi, and orange roughy.

ORANGE ROUGHY WITH MUSHROOMS AND OLIVES
(Serves 4)

- ☐ 4 fillets of orange roughy
- ☐ 8 ounces mushrooms, sliced
- ☐ 1 small onion, chopped
- ☐ 2 heaping tablespoons all-purpose flour
- ☐ 1 lemon
- ☐ 4 ounces olives (green, black, or stuffed)
- ☐ 1 tablespoon oil or butter
- ☐ A dash Worcestershire sauce to taste
- ☐ Salt and pepper to taste

Chop the olives (not too small). Put the fish fillets on a platter. Season them with salt, pepper and Worcestershire sauce. Warm up a large frying pan with the oil. Dust the fillets with flour. Fry them in the pan until golden brown. Flip them over. When brown on both sides, lift them gently and put them on the platter. Put the platter in a preheated oven, 175 to 200 degrees, max. Toss the onion in the pan that you took the fillet out of. When soft-cooked, add the mushrooms and cook 2 to 3 more minutes. Add the chopped olives. Squeeze the lemon juice over it. (If you squeeze the lemon juice over a sieve, you won't have to pick out the pits.) Toss for one minute or so and spread over the fish fillets. Serve hot.

POACHED COD (Serves 4)

- ☐ 4 fillets of cod, 6 to 8 ounces each
- ☐ 1 small onion, sliced
- ☐ 1 to 2 carrots, sliced
- ☐ 6 garlic cloves
- ☐ 1 to 2 celery stalks, sliced or chopped
- ☐ 1 bay leaf
- ☐ 2 tablespoons white vinegar
- ☐ Salt to taste
- ☐ 1 pinch thyme
- ☐ 4 large ripe tomatoes, diced
- ☐ 1 lemon or lemon juice
- ☐ Salt to taste

On the stove put a pan with 4 cups water. Slice the onion, celery and carrot (not too small). Put it all in the water along with the 2 whole garlic cloves, bay leaf, a pinch of salt, and 2 tablespoons vinegar. Bring it to a boil and simmer 15 to 20 minutes. Dice the tomato into ½-inch cubes. Chop the remaining 4 cloves of garlic. Put the tomato, garlic, and thyme in a pan. Cook at medium heat for 8 to 10 minutes. Leave it covered on the side of the range until the fish is poached.

Put the fish in a large frying pan or a high baking sheet. Pour the broth over the fish without the vegetables. Bake 10 to 12 minutes in a preheated oven at 375 degrees.

The tomato puree from the frying pan must be divided into 4 equal parts on 4 plates. Put the poached fish delicately on top of the tomato bed. Drain the fillet well as you take out each piece. Decorate each fillet with a lemon wedge or put a bottle of lemon juice on the table to sprinkle on the fish, if necessary.

PAN-FRIED SALMON WITH MUSHROOMS

- ☐ 4 slices of salmon, about 6 to 8 ounces each
- ☐ 1 to 2 heaping tablespoons flour
- ☐ 1 small onion, sliced
- ☐ 2 tablespoons regular oil
- ☐ ¼ teaspoon thyme
- ☐ ½ small lemon, peeled and chopped
- ☐ 1 pound sliced mushrooms
- ☐ 2 lemons
- ☐ Whole parsley to taste
- ☐ Salt and pepper to taste
- ☐ A dash Worcestershire sauce to taste

Preheat oven at 350 to 375 degrees. Put approximately 1 tablespoon oil in a frying pan. Heat it up (hot, but not smoking). Sprinkle the salmon with flour on both sides and dust off the excess. Put the 4 salmon steaks in the frying pan and cook until brown. Flip them over and repeat. When brown on both sides, put the salmon steaks on a cookie sheet, squeeze the juice of one lemon over them, and slide them into the oven.

Wipe the frying pan with a paper towel. Add the rest of the oil (1 tablespoon), the sliced onion, and the thyme and cook for 4 to 5 minutes until soft. Add the mushrooms and cook another 5 minutes. Then add a pinch of salt, a small amount of pepper, a dash of Worcestershire sauce, and the peeled and chopped lemon.

By now the salmon is cooked, so take it out of the oven. Put the steaks on plates, with the mushroom sauce on top. Serve hot after having decorated with a lemon wedge and fresh parsley. *Et voila*! Serve with new potatoes (steamed) or even an array of vegetables.

GARLIC CHICKEN

This is one of my favorites, and it does not come any easier. Wash one whole chicken in cold water and dry it with a paper towel. Put salt and pepper and rub thyme inside and outside. One whole head of garlic is required also, which you will hold between the finger and the thumb. Cut the garlic horizontally between the root and the start of the stem. Shove all halves into the chicken cavity and place it in a metal ovenproof pan. Rub the breast and legs with your favorite oil. There it is. You are just about finished. Now the chicken must go into a preheated oven at 425 degrees for approximately 45 minutes. It will be crisp and golden brown. Discard the garlic. Serve with mashed potatoes (page 97), chicken gravy (page 31), and Brussels sprouts (page 98).

Remember, don't bother peeling the garlic.

LEFTOVERS : Pull chicken from the bone and chop the meat into large chunks. Put it into a bowl with a couple of teaspoons of mayonnaise and mix. It makes a great sandwich.

TARRAGON CHICKEN (Serves 4)

- 4 boned chicken breasts
- 2 tablespoons flour
- 4 tablespoons oil
- 1 teaspoon tarragon
- 1 packet brown gravy
- Salt and pepper to taste

Preheat a frying pan with the oil. When the frying pan is hot, lightly dust the chicken breasts with flour. (Do not dust the breasts ahead of time. It will create a crust, resulting in chewy meat). Cook both sides until golden brown. For the gravy, follow the instructions on the package. Add the tarragon. *Bon appetit.*

CHICKEN BASQUE (Serves 4)

- ☐ 1 whole chicken, cut unto pieces (substitute 4 thighs and 4 drumsticks, if you like)
- ☐ 2 pounds tomatoes, diced, or 2 large cans of diced tomatoes
- ☐ 4 tablespoons flour
- ☐ 3 tablespoons butter
- ☐ 2 whole onions, sliced
- ☐ 2 garlic cloves, cleaned, chopped, and crushed
- ☐ 1 can tomato sauce (6 to 8 ounces)
- ☐ 1 tablespoon chopped parsley (fresh or dry)
- ☐ 8 ounces green pepper, chopped
- ☐ ½ teaspoon thyme
- ☐ Salt and pepper to taste

Put half the butter in a frying pan. Dust the chicken pieces with the flour and put them in the pan. Cook 35 minutes at low heat. In a different pan, put the rest of the butter, together with the onions, green pepper and thyme. Cook 10 minutes at low heat. Add the diced tomatoes and garlic and simmer another 5 minutes. Blend the chicken with the sauce. Add salt and pepper. Five more minutes will do the trick. Put the sauce on a platter with the chicken on top. Sprinkle with the chopped parsley.
Rice or pasta is an excellent compliment. You can add black olives, celery, or capers for variations.

CHICKEN BREASTS WITH BLACKBERRY SAUCE

- ☐ 4 large chicken breasts (for the healthy appetite, make that 2 per person)
- ☐ 2 heaping tablespoons flour
- ☐ 2 large whole eggs
- ☐ 1 pack plain bread crumbs
- ☐ 1 pinch salt

- ☐ 4 ounces oil
- ☐ Unsweetened coconut (1 small package)

Mix the bread crumbs with the unsweetened coconut. Whisk the eggs in a large bowl with a pinch of salt. Put the flour on a platter and spread it out. Flour the chicken breast lightly on each side. As you dust the chicken breast, shake off the excess flour. Discard the leftover flour. Put the chicken breasts in the bowl with the egg and turn them very gently until they are moist all over. The flour will make the egg wash stick. Now put the bread crumbs mixed with the coconut in a platter or a cake pan with a high rim of 2 inches or more. Take a chicken breast and hold it up a couple of seconds to drain the excess egg wash. Put it in the bread crumbs and cover it well with the crumbs. Pound the chicken breast gently but firmly. Flip the chicken breast over. Do it again. It will seal the meat well. Pick it up gently and shake off the excess crumbs. Put it on a plate and repeat the process with each piece of chicken.

Put the frying pan on the stove with the oil and heat it up. Put a stirring wooden spoon in the oil. When the wood starts making bubbles, it is hot enough to start cooking. Cook the chicken breasts on each side until golden brown. Depending on the size of your frying pan, cook 2, 3, or 4 at the same time. Put the chicken breasts on a cookie sheet in a preheated oven at 350 degrees for 10 minutes. Discard the oil.

BLACKBERRY SAUCE

- ☐ 1 pack brown gravy
- ☐ 2 to 3 teaspoons blackberry preserves

Cook the gravy according to the directions. Whisk the blackberry preserves into the gravy. You can replace half of the water from the suggested amount on the package with red wine. One tablespoon or so of whipping cream can be mixed in the gravy during cooking to make it more velvety.

CHICKEN THIGHS WITH QUICK CURRY SAUCE

Count 1 to 2 thighs per lady, and 2 to 3 for the gentlemen, or in my case, make it 4 per man. However, let's get back to our chicken.

- ☐ 8 thighs (breasts or drumsticks will also do)
- ☐ 1 cup white wine (optional, but better) or 1 cup water
- ☐ 2 chicken bouillon cubes
- ☐ 4 ounces low-fat sour cream or yogurt

Now the next ingredients are totally optional. Do not panic. It will turn out as the best curry chicken ever. I promise. Look up in your cupboards or in the fridge for orange juice, apples, coconut shavings, sliced almonds, bananas, a can of peaches, cherry preserves, pineapple (fresh or canned), raisins, pitted prunes, or dates. You see how it will go; now how to put it together.

First, warm up a frying pan with high sides, or a large cooking pan. Put the oil in it. Sprinkle the chicken pieces with flour and shake off the excess. Put them in the pan. Sauté for about 3 to 4 minutes, until golden brown. Flip them over and repeat the process. Reduce the heat to low. Add one cup of wine or one cup of water and the chicken bouillon cubes. Cover it with a lid and simmer 12 to 15 minutes. When cooked, add 1 to 2 teaspoons of curry, depending on your taste. Add 1 cup orange juice (could be substituted with grape, pineapple, peach, or apple juices — trust me). Bring it to a boil. Sprinkle the remaining flour all over the chicken. Chop the apple and add it to the pan with the sour cream (or any flavor yogurt). Add the raisins, peaches, or pineapple. Add the sliced almonds or coconut, pitted prunes (chopped), dates, or sliced banana. Simmer 3 to 4 minutes. Stir gently. Add a tiny bit of salt, if required. Add more curry if you like it stronger. For change of flavor, a spoon of cherry preserves or even orange preserves is excellent. You will have a spicy sweet, becoming the talk of your guests for a long time. Serve with rice.

Another easy dish you can prepare quickly (serves 4 to 6):

- ☐ 8 drumsticks
- ☐ 8 meatballs
- ☐ 4 sausages, smoked or fresh
- ☐ ½ cup fresh parsley, chopped
- ☐ 2 cups rice
- ☐ 4 cups water
- ☐ 4 bouillon cubes

Cook the chicken drumsticks to a golden brown. In a pre-greased oven sauté pan put the rice, chicken drumsticks, water and bouillon cubes. Cook 15 minutes in a preheated oven at 425 to 450 degrees. Add the sausage and precooked meatballs (the Swedish or Italian ones from your freezer) and cook another 10 minutes. Serve hot.

For variety you can add one or two cups of broccoli together with the rice or chicken, or a can of tomato puree, or sliced or whole mushrooms. You can replace drumsticks with pieces of chicken breast or thighs. Even pork cutlets will do; or forget the chicken sausage and just increase the meat balls (cook only the last 10 minutes).

You can also dice a can of peaches in rice to be served with a curry or venison dish (for hunters) or a can of Bing cherry or tangerine segments for a dish of chicken breast in coconut blackberry sauce (see Sauces).

THE TOUR

I had my own catering company doing a lot of extra special requests for anniversaries, showers, baptisms, and other occasions too numerous to mention. One day I got a phone call from a gentleman.

"Are you François?"

"Yes, sir."

"I have heard a lot of good things about you."

"How nice."

"Listen, I need a cake for eighty people."

"No problem. Which flavor would you like?"

"It does not matter. Just get me a cake for eighty people. Nothing fancy." He gave me the date which left me three days to prepare it.

"Where do you want it delivered?"

"At the Skydome."

"You mean downtown at the new stadium."

"Yes."

"Care of. . .?"

"The Rolling Stones Steel Wheel Tour."

I nearly dropped the phone. He must be joking — a simple slab of cake, any flavor. "Whom do I bill for it?"

"Make it out to The Rolling Stones Steel Wheel Tour, care of me." He gave me his name, a phone number where to reach him, a place and a time to deliver the cake.

Wow! I had a request for a cake. Of all the people in the world, it was for the Rolling Stones, and they wanted it simple. My choice! It took me a day to debate on a variety of delicacies. Finally, I came up with a simple enough solution: Italian cream cake.

For decoration I made the Canadian flag with two strips of marzipan (an almond paste) on each side and a maple leaf in the middle, and I made a logo of their "sticky finger" emblem all along the border. Needless to say, I was punctual for my appointment, excited like a six-year-old waiting for his first pony ride. The security people asked the nature of my business. "I have to deliver a cake for the Rolling Stones," I said.

"We have been notified. This way, please." Within minutes a gentleman came to greet me. I gave him the bill.

"Will cash be satisfactory?"

"Cash is fine." I waited a few seconds as he looked over the bill and asked, "Is there any chance to meet any member of the group?"

"I am afraid it is out of the question. We have so many requests, it would be an inconvenience for them if we granted them all, so we prefer to deny all demands. Have a nice day." I never got to meet the Rolling Stones. So much for my pony ride.

Desserts

SWISS APPLE PIE

This is my mother's recipe and it is time you tried her delicacy.

- ☐ 6 apples (cooking apples are best)
- ☐ 1 deep-dish pie shell from your grocer's freezer
- ☐ ¼ teaspoon cinnamon
- ☐ Juice from 1 lemon to taste
- ☐ 5 heaping tablespoons sugar
- ☐ 4 eggs
- ☐ 2 cups milk
- ☐ A dash vanilla extract to taste

Preheat the oven to 375 degrees. Peel and remove the cores from the apples; cut them in wedges, each apple making 8 slices. Put them in a large bowl together with 1 heaping tablespoon sugar (more or less), the lemon juice, and the cinnamon. Mix well. Put the apple mixture into the pie shell. Spread it evenly without flattening it. Put it in the oven and bake for 15 minutes. Whisk together the milk, vanilla extract, and the rest of the sugar and pour it over the pie. Reduce the heat to 325 degrees and bake for another 15 minutes, or until the contents are firm. Let it sit and cool off for 20 to 30 minutes before cutting and serving. Serve with whipped cream (optional).

CHERRY PIE IN CUSTARD

> Any dried beans that you have in your kitchen can be used when baking a pie shell to keep it from becoming misshapen.

- ☐ 1 deep-dish pie shell from your grocer's freezer
- ☐ 1 can sour pitted Bing cherries
- ☐ 4 eggs
- ☐ ½ tablespoon brandy or cherry brandy
- ☐ 3 heaping tablespoons sugar
- ☐ ½ teaspoon cornstarch
- ☐ 2 cups milk
- ☐ 1 pound dried kidney beans, lima beans, or black-eyed peas (to keep the shape of the pie crust while it bakes)

Preheat the oven to 350 degrees. Take the pie shell out of the freezer. Put the dried beans in and cook in the oven for 15 minutes. In the meantime, whisk together the eggs, sugar and milk in a bowl and set it aside. Drain the can of cherries, pressing gently to remove most of the juice and catching the juice in a pan. Cook the juice at medium heat until it is reduced to approximately half its volume. Add one teaspoon sugar. Take the pie out of the oven and remove the dried beans. Put the drained cherries in the form. Gently pour the egg and sugar mixture all over it.

Put it back in the oven on a cookie sheet to prevent spillage and bake for approximately 20 to 30 minutes, or until the custard is cooked. Mix the corn starch and brandy with a fork in a small cup or butter dish. Pour it slowly into the cherry juice while whisking. Set it aside to cool off a bit. Take out the pie and let it sit 15 minutes.

Put a couple of tablespoons of sauce in the bottom of a plate. Put a slice of cherry custard on top of it. Put one more spoon of cherry gravy on top of the pie, but only on half of it (it looks better that way).

If calories are not an issue, serve with a spoon (or 5) of freshly whipped cream.

BAKED APPLES IN RED WINE

- ☐ 4 large firm apples (Cooking apples are best. Produce managers can be very helpful and should know or be willing to make a suggestion.)
- ☐ 2 to 4 ounces walnut pieces
- ☐ 4 heaping tablespoons brown sugar
- ☐ 1 teaspoon butter
- ☐ 2 cups red wine
- ☐ 1 heaping tablespoon cornstarch
- ☐ 1 pinch cinnamon (powder or a small stick)
- ☐ Juice from 1 lemon or 1 tablespoon prepared juice

Core the apples. Poke the apple skins all over with a knife or fork. Put the apples in a baking dish. Fill the hole with the walnuts. It doesn't matter if part of the walnuts fall beside the apples. Sprinkle brown sugar all over the apples and the pan (1 heaping tablespoon sugar per apple). Put one dab of butter on top of each apple. Pour the 2 cups of wine in the pan. If you use a cinnamon stick, put it in the wine. Bake the apples until soft, about 20 to 30 minutes, depending on the size of your fruit. When done, put each apple on an individual dessert plate and let it cool for 10 minutes. Save the juice from the pan.

In the meantime, put the wine and apple juice from the pan in a small cooking pan and bring it to a boil. Mix the cornstarch with 1 tablespoon water. Whisk it slowly into the red wine. Be careful; the red wine sauce should have the consistency of maple syrup, so pour it in slowly. Squeeze on the lemon juice and a pinch of cinnamon. Serve it on the side in a gravy boat.

Tips For Entertaining

TIPS FOR ENTERTAINING

Composing a menu is not too difficult, providing you follow a few basic rules. First, the season is important for availability and freshness of ingredients. Second, you must take into consideration the occasion. You never need a reason for a good meal — besides just eating for the sake of eating. For example, there are anniversaries, birthdays, business dinners, etc. Find out in whose honor the dinner will be served, and cater to his or her taste preference, religious background, or allergy medical restrictions. If it is a surprise, ask the spouse or children, or secretary for the necessary information. There are many ways to do it.

Next, make a list of how many guests are going to be present. Make your guest list in accordance with your budget. It makes no sense to pay for a wedding for the next twenty years. You could invite only the immediate family for dinner, asking the rest of the guests to join on a separate invitation to a garden toast of white wine and light *hors d'oeuvres*.

You can cut the cost of entertaining considerably by planning a potpourri which you call pot luck dinners. With groups of friends and/or family everyone brings something, but don't tell people to "just bring anything." You might end up with twenty congealed salads. It is perfectly all right to take charge and say, "Coleslaw. I have no coleslaw." or "A plate of cookies would be perfect." How about, "The chicken dish you made at John's birthday last year was superb." If you make the decision, you will have less confusion, better variety, and everyone will love you for it.

When there is any formal event like a wedding, there is bound to be confusion. Men are restless and regular meals are often forgotten, so ask your close friend — not the maid of honor or the mother of the bride, but someone close — to make a huge plate of sandwiches well covered with Saran wrap, and a tub of potato salad. You will probably have out-of-town guests with children or men coming to ask you one hour before the ceremony, "Is there anything to eat?" just as you are about to do the last touch-up on your hair.

So answer kindly, "Look in the fridge. There is a plate of sandwiches and potato salad. Now, run along!" You see, it is so easy! Of course, the same applies for anniversaries, baptisms, and most special occasions.

PERSONALITY OF THE MENU

Now, this subject is of great importance for mixed gatherings or marriages of different ethnic or religious beliefs. Sometimes it causes days of argument, making one lose focus of the real occasion. If it is for a birthday, find out what the birthday person prefers, wants, or fancies. It is their day, so please them — not each guest. It is the same rule for all gatherings. On a Golden Anniversary, we should concentrate on the happy couple, not try to please each individual. It is too complicated.

One day an undercover police officer asked me about doing a surprise party for his best friend at his friend's own house. I was to bring all the food, rental employees, and games without the friend being there, although he hardly ever left home except to go to work. This is what we came up with.

The police officer called up his buddy and said, "My wife has left me. She went back home telling me I have neglected her and have been working too much." He sounded sad and upset, ready to commit an act he would regret. Needless to say, his friend came right over to console him in his difficult moment. Our undercover officer stretched the time into four hours. "I don't want to stay at home alone," he said to his friend.

"Well, come on over to my place." Guess what a surprise it was when he walked in his door and saw all of his friends standing there with the house fully decorated! You see, it is worth investing time and a little legwork for a dear friend.

NUMBER OF GUESTS

If you can cater, well, obviously do so and you can let the pro do the job. If it is a romantic dinner for two, you will want a more personal touch and can be a bit more elaborate. Keep in mind you can go and purchase a few dishes at your local gourmet outlet. For a party of six to ten I would not advise more than three courses, the reason being that you must also converse, entertain, serve the drinks, and still look calm and collected. So keep it simple. Do as much as possible the day before.

THE PORTIONS

If you have a sit-down dinner of three plates you must reduce the filler (rice, potatoes, pasta). Your guests would like to enjoy each one of your creations and will by choice disregard the filler mentioned above.

For prepared meat like chicken breasts or roast steak, allow 6 to 8 ounces per person. For chicken (bone in), pork chops, or back ribs, allow 8 to 12 ounces per person. For duck, turkey, or leg of lamb you must count 12 to 16 ounces per person. For vegetables, 3 ounce per person is usually sufficient. For starches like potatoes, rice, and noodles, 2½ to 3 ounces is plenty with a main dish. For a main course like Fettuccine Alfredo, Penne Primavera, or chicken and rice casseroles, you must count 5 ounces per person, cooked.

ORDER OF SERVING

Hors d'oeuvres (appetizers), main course, and dessert is the classic order. Do not feel you have to serve all dishes quickly. Consider serving the appetizer in the living room while all your guests are getting acquainted or catching up on the latest gossip. You can follow by asking them to join you in the dining room for the main course. Ask your spouse to take the guests into the den while you clear up the table and reset it for dessert .

Food is not a gobbling contest but rather a social event. Take your time. You will make less mistakes and reduce the stress level. If you forget or miss something, don't mention it. The chances are that no one else will notice.

If by any chance you have mentioned the menu to some of your guests and you were unable to make it or it was overcooked and not presentable, again, don't worry. If they insist like, "I thought we were going to have salmon," your answer could be, "I had a divine Cabernet fitting the texture of chicken." or "The salmon would not have done honor to this table. It was not as fresh as I expected. I opted for the fresh scallops," or "Why salmon? I had a craving for chicken *picatas*."

A good wine is always a compliment to a good meal. As a rule, most people enjoy red wine with red meat, and white wine with white meat and fish. Red wine is for spicy food, white wine for delicate dishes, and rose or blush for lamb. If you serve two or more wines, the white should be first, followed by the fuller body red variety. Now, these are simple rules. It gets more complicated if you are an expert. Here we deal in simple, easy generalities and having fun.

Never push a friend who is driving to have a drink. If they start to lean heavily on the bottle, say simply, "Dinner will be served shortly, and I have cooked it specially for you. If you drink too much, you won't be able to taste it and my feelings will be hurt. Now behave yourself, Darling." Have plenty of coffee, regular and decaf, as well as ice and cold drinks. Call a cab if necessary or have them sleep on the couch. It prevents accidents.

Preparation and organization can be done after you have established the number of guests, ethnic backgrounds, and monetary restrictions. Then you choose the menu, check your spice cabinet, freezer, and pantry. Check on special seasonal vegetables, and write your menu.

The best dinners are the ones you remember years after for the good company and great food.

MAKE A LIST

If possible, ask your butcher to prepare the portions of beef, pork, veal, or lamb and to de-bone and string up the roast. Remember their motto, "We are here to help." Choose your fruit and vegetables carefully. Prepare as many dishes as possible 24 to 48 hours in advance.

Do not choose a complicated menu. Do not try new recipes (if you insist, I am getting out of the kitchen). Before the event, prepare the table and put a light cloth over it as a dust cover. You will have plenty of other chores the day of the event.

On the day of the event, stop at least once every hour to check your list of what needs to be done next. It is the best way to be ready on time.

PLAN AHEAD

Around the holidays one often gets caught in a bind from last minute changes in plans, extra guests arriving on short notice, or forgetting to accommodate special diets of our guests. So, here are a few quick tips for the holidays that will give you extra time to shop for presents, give a light dusting to the house, take a shower, or even take a few minutes' breather for yourself.

Whenever you go to the grocery store, make a point to walk by the delicatessen and make a mental list (or if you have a mind as feeble as mine, take notes on a piece of paper). Large towns and cities have better selections than small rural hamlets. Here are a few items I found in an Austin grocery store: fresh chicken, cilantro sausage, garlic hot sausage, ostrich patties (believe me, they make the best meat sauce you can imagine), green pasta salad, vegetable bacon salad, Aztec salad, potato and bacon salad, penne con Pico salad, stuffed salmon (all you have to do is add the light mustard and dill sauce with a vegetable or salad), stuffed pork chops, marinated lemon grass chicken breast, Cajun marinated catfish, meat of vegetable *emponadas*, various pastas, vegetarian lasagna, and stuffed Cornish hen (good with black currant sauce). The list goes on, so have their phone numbers handy. Phone ahead to have your grocer prepare it for you.

If the party is of special importance, get someone to help in the kitchen or someone to assist in serving. Better yet, get both. Your cleaning lady may need the extra cash or get out the Yellow Pages and look under catering companies. Have them come two to three hours prior to the event so you can brief them. You will feel more confident if they learn beforehand where to find everything.

Always have 1 to 2 pounds of gourmet coffee in the freezer.

Have a couple of different desserts in the freezer. A pie or a frozen meringue ice cream cake or gourmet ice cream will do in a pinch.

Keep two or three bottles of white and red wine (remember, don't let your guests drink and drive; you don't want your guests to have a mishap on the way home).

Don't worry about the dirty dishes. There will be plenty of time to soak or wash them later. Besides, dishes make noise. Your guests want to see you — not talk to your back in the kitchen. Have time set aside the next morning to clean up the kitchen.

Have a couple of extra blankets for guests who drink too much. It is better if he or she spends the night on your couch if necessary. Or call a cab and offer to pay for it. Have regular strong coffee available in addition to decaf.

If your guest eats too much, which is often the case (even for me), offer a natural enzyme or a cold soda. It speeds up the digestive process.

Fresh flowers are not always a must on the table. Many bushes produce colorful berries during the cold months. Add a nice porcelain figurine or candles, and you have an original centerpiece. Just remember to keep it low so you can easily see your guests. Here is one final thought until the next time, Take care of the cook!

FINI

(Until next time may the power of good taste be with you!)

TO OUR READERS . . .

Hopefully this book will inspire your creativity. Your experiences, both your joys and sorrows, in the kitchen are of great interest to the author and Averette Publications, Inc. Remember the comedies and tragedies enacted in the heart of the house, write them down, and share them with us.

Your thoughts, things in the book that worked well for you and those that didn't, and suggestions for improvement in future books are welcome. First and foremost, what do you think of this book? In addition, we would love to hear about your successes and failures in the kitchen. You may have a question about cooking that you have been unable to get answered. Give Master Chef François the opportunity to solve your dilemma.

Just make a copy of the next page and send it to Averette Publications, Inc., PO Box 685069, Austin, Texas 78768, or use the form on our website to email your comments to us.

Thanks in advance for your thoughts and ideas, and please stay in touch!

Comments:

Name:

Address:

You have my permission to quote from my comments, and use these quotations in ads, brochures, mail, publications and other promotions.

Signed: Date:

TO ORDER ADDITIONAL COPIES
1-800-487-6093
http://www.treasurebook.com

ABOUT THE AUTHOR . . .

François Sigrist was born and educated in Geneva, Switzerland. His professional education in Classical French Cuisine was completed with a three-year apprenticeship at the Hotel de la Paix et Hotel Strasbourg et Univer under the tutorage of Master Chef Paul Gautey. He later became the youngest chef to be inducted into the World Federation of Master Chefs.

He lived in Canada for more than twenty years where he worked for a major food corporation and also founded his own restaurant with his brother. During these years he cooked for many dignitaries and celebrities, including Queen Elizabeth, the Rolling Stones, Ronald Reagan, Frank Miller, Paul Newman, Warren Beatty, Isaac Hays, Barry White, etc., and for seven years he did a cooking segment twice a month on CFTO-TV, Channel 9, in Toronto. In the past year he has appeared on numerous morning and noon shows on local cable, CBS, NBC, FOX, and ABC affiliates.

Through the years his peers and fans urged him to write a cookbook. His answer to their requests was that there were already too many cookbooks on the shelves. In fact his idea was to put out a cookbook with one printed page of instructions. On that page would be two words, "Make Reservations".

From his travels and experiences over the last eight years, he was inspired to write a fictional novel with positive attitudes and solutions aimed at the universal problems of the homeless. He recently completed a 16-state book signing tour on his Kawasaki motorcycle during which he discovered that the public had a genuine interest in his talents when they read in the press releases that he was a master chef. Children of the baby boomers, he observed, were viewing cooking as a lost art and seeking professional guidance.

The lack of interest, respect, and creative freedom that had pushed him away from his first love of cooking has reversed and drawn him back as the expert who knows the basics–an expert who desires to de-mystify and simplify the culinary arts. Master Chef François has answered the requests of his avid fans and written volume one ***Basic Rules and Shortcuts*** in a series of cookbooks entitled ***Secrets Of A Master Chef.*** One of the greatest secrets is that French cooking is simple, and François can show the reader how to use shortcuts to create culinary delights.

INDEX OF RECIPES

Alphabetical

Notes

Notes

Notes

Notes

Notes

Notes